Poverty and Anti-Poverty Strategy

GW00836249

Response

A study of the development of anti-poverty strategy in metropolitan authorities

By Susan Balloch and Brian Jones

 Association of Metropolitan Authorities

THE ASSOCIATION OF METROPOLITAN AUTHORITIES represents the 36 metropolitan districts councils, 30 London boroughs, the City of London, and the Inner London Education Authority. Corporate membership is also open to the Joint Authorities responsible for Police, Fire and Civil Defence, and Passenger Transport.

The Association's principal role is to promote and protect the interests of its member authorities and the communities they serve in the constant round of negotiations that takes place with central government, its Departments and national organisations.

Whenever possible it acts on the basis of a political consensus within its own ranks and in concert with the other local authority Associations. In all its activities it takes as its fundamental principle the belief that democratically elected authorities are the best judge of needs and priorities in the areas which they serve.

Association of Metropolitan Authorities
35 Great Smith Street
London SW1P 3BJ
01-222 8100

Poverty and Anti-Poverty Strategy:
The Local Government Response

Produced by the Association of Metropolitan Authorities. £7·50
1st Edition and Imprint March 1990
© AMA 1990
ISBN 0 902052 76 4

Contents

Acknowledgements

Many people have given help and encouragement to this project. In particular we should like to thank Toby Harris who chaired our steering group so effectively and officiated at many extra meetings. Our appreciation goes also to the members of the steering group, including Saul Becker, Geoff Fimister, Ruth Lister, Jane Streather, Sue Wainwright and Gill Witting. David Wells and John Barnes, who also were members of the steering group, enabled us to pilot our survey in Southwark and we are grateful to them for their friendly support. Likewise we wish to thank Richard Harbord and his staff in Richmond for allowing Richmond to be piloted as a control for the survey.

We could not have attempted this survey without the co-operation and help of the forty-one metropolitan authorities who participated in it and their liaison officers. It is impossible to mention them all by name but their hard work and commitment to anti-poverty strategy is fully recognised. Birmingham, Bolton, Kirklees and Manchester hosted meetings on special topics and we thank them for their help and advice. We were extremely pleased to have received the support of those councillors who were able to attend our regional meetings.

Within the AMA itself our thanks must go to all those members of the Secretariat who gave us specialist advice within their own fields of expertise and to Jean Dawes, Ruth Gregory and the other members of the word processing team whose skills took us through many revisions. The Public Relations Department designed and produced this publication, giving us many helpful hints on the way and we thank them too.

Responsibility for the outcome is, of course, entirely ours.

Susan Balloch
Brian Jones   March 1989

Preface

In 1984, the Social Services Committee of the Association of Metropolitan Authorities approved research into the impact of unemployment on the demand for personal social services. The report, *Caring for Unemployed People* which was subsequently published in 1985, revealed not only extensive poverty amongst the most vulnerable groups of people regularly using the social services but also a new group of 'poor clients' driven to seek assistance with financial problems. The implications of this research coupled with concern following the passing of the 1986 Social Security Act, encouraged the Social Services Committee to undertake a more wide-ranging research and development programme into the impact of poverty across all local government services. Although biased towards the responses of social services departments, this research was conceived within a broad framework in which housing, education, economic development and planning, public protection, leisure and chief executive's departments were all seen as important respondents, as well as regional passenger transport and fire authorities.

The steering group created to mastermind the research agreed that the work should fall into two stages. The first stage, which commenced in January 1987 and was completed in March 1988, involved the piloting and subsequent circulation of a lengthy questionnaire to all key local government departments. Fifty-six of the Association's sixty-seven members expressed their willingness to complete this questionnaire and forty-one were ultimately able to do so. The results have been presented over the last eighteen months in various papers and articles in other publications, including the *Municipal Review*, and are now drawn together in this short book. They have formed the basis for a discussion of poverty and anti-poverty strategy in local government, which is likely to continue at least until the end of the century. The second stage involved a series of case studies of specific issues in anti-poverty strategy, including economic and social regeneration, targeting, fees and charges, credit unions and debt collection. An anti-poverty working group consisting of a small number of authorities met every two months between June 1988 and September 1989, each time in a different authority, to discuss these issues and hear how officers and councillors in the host authority were addressing them. This provided both the local colour and in-depth discussions lacking in the survey's postal questionnaires.

The period 1987 to 1989 has clearly been one of unusually rapid change in local government. Major new legislation affecting local government finance, including the introduction in 1990 of the community charge, housing, education, social services and economic development activity is changing the whole environment in which local government operates, with a consequent, drastic reduction in both local government's levels of expenditure and numbers of employees and a contraction of direct service provision. Conducting research in such a climate was a challenging and difficult task, but perhaps doubly important at the same time, given that concern for the poor was mounting too. Evidence from official statistics of an increasingly divided Britain, as demonstrated by Halsey's introduction to the 1987 edition of *Social Trends*, was supplemented by a range of evidence used in this text. Voluntary groups, academic bodies and local government itself illustrated the problems being faced by a wide range of impoverished groups of people, particularly the homeless, single parent families, disabled and elderly people and their carers, mentally ill people, children leaving care and unemployed young people. Most studies recognised that women and members of ethnic minorities figured disproportionately amongst those in need. Changing legislation and evidence of increasing poverty is now challenging those in charge of local government to re-evaluate their priorities and the methods in use for realising these priorities. Anti-poverty strategies are evolving in increasing numbers to embrace this difficult task. They have to ensure that, in the 1990s, those most in need of local government services will not become, or in some cases continue to be, the losers. Nor should services for them be marginalised.

This study reviews some of the methods through which knowledge of patterns of local poverty is developing and anti-poverty strategies are emerging. Chapter Two concentrates on practical ways of creating local authority 'poverty profiles'. Chapter Three reviews the development of anti-poverty strategies in a number of the metropolitan authorities. Chapter Four focuses on some of the issues which have emerged as most important in anti-poverty in the course of the AMA research. Because this project was initiated by the AMA's Social Services Committee, Chapter Five concentrates on the particular implications of anti-poverty strategy for some aspects of social services departments. It is hoped that, in due course, similar discussions will be developed on housing, education, economic development, leisure, transport and health. Meanwhile the continuation of this research and development work has been made possible through the generous support of individual authorities and with the backing of the AMA's Policy Committee.

Chapter Six is intended to stand on its own as a discussion paper on anti-poverty strategy. It could be used for a local authority's in-house debate or any local seminar. While outlining practical steps that can be taken towards the implementation of a strategy it recognises the challenge likely to be presented by the 1990s. In particular it notes the difficulties that may be created for people on low incomes by the introduction of the community charge (poll tax) in April 1990 (see Appendix 3), the extension of compulsory competitive tendering, the implementation of the Griffiths' Report on Community Care, the effects of the 1988 Education Reform Act, of recent major legislation in Housing and of the 1986 Social Security Act and subsequent changes in levels of benefit.

As this text demonstrates, however, there are good grounds for believing that, with determination and imagination, local authorities will be able to develop successful anti-poverty strategies in the next decade, particularly if they work together with the other local institutions. International develop-ments may help rather than hinder this process. In particular the thinking which led to the European Social Charter may broaden attempts to analyse, understand and alleviate poverty. The Third European Programme to Combat Poverty has just been launched and, although under-resourced, promises a more stimulating forum for the evaluation of anti-poverty strategy than has hitherto been the case. Though undoubtedly fraught with difficulty, the future is alive with the hope that not only new concerns, but also fresh knowledge and greater opportunities, will encourage professional and practical approaches to poverty. Of course, this book raises many important questions which can be dealt with only by a combination of determined political and administrative action. Much of this rests with national government. In the last decade national policies have made poverty worse and, at the same time, limited local authorities' efforts to protect their local communities. Local authorities are committed to developing significant opportunities for action even if the national political determination is lacking. With a stronger national commitment, the local authorities could play an even more important role in the battle against poverty.

Toby Harris

I Poverty and Local Government

1. Responsibility for poverty

At the beginning of 1987 the Social Services Committee of the Association of Metropolitan Authorities (AMA) launched a new initiative in poverty research. This aimed to look at the impact of poverty on local authority services and the responses being made to support and improve the living conditions of those on low incomes. Mounting concern in the AMA about evidence of increasing poverty was justified by its earlier study of the impact of unemployment on social services departments published in 1985 (*Balloch et al*). From the limited concentration in this study on the effects of unemployment on a few user groups in social services departments, research was extended to the broader concept of poverty and to the impact of this on a wider range of local authority services.

The complexity of this investigation was acknowledged from the outset. Poverty is an evaluative term. Its definition has always been problematic and the extent to which it should be considered in 'absolute' or 'relative' terms remains a source of confusion in the study of incomes and needs (*Ringen and Donnison, 1988*). In the AMA study emphasis has been placed on both 'income poverty', that is lack of monetary resources resulting from unemployment, low pay and inadequate benefits, and on 'relative deprivation' resulting from the lack of those basic material and social resources that enable individuals to participate normally in everyday life (*Townsend et al, 1987*). In addition, it was acknowledged that poverty is characterised by the 'powerlessness' of those affected. The Archbishop of Canterbury's introduction to *Faith in the City* (1986) argued that 'Poor people . . . are at the mercy of fragmented and apparently unresponsive public authorities. They are trapped in housing and in environments over which they have little control. They lack the means and opportunity – which so many of us take for granted – of making choices in their lives.' Lack of money, lack of resources and lack of control were thus the three dimensions to be explored within the context of this research.

A punitive approach characterised government policy towards the poor throughout the nineteenth century but the first half of the twentieth century witnessed a redefinition of the responsibilities of the state towards poor people which crystallised in Beveridge's use of the concept of the 'national minimum'. Beveridge's translation of Rowntree's calculations on the income necessary to sustain physical efficiency into, for example, pensions, children's allowances and national assistance created the basis on which social security has subsequently developed (*Thane, 1986*). In spite of extensive changes involving, in particular, a return to means testing and a growing emphasis on voluntary and private sources of welfare, the fact that central government is ultimately responsible for maintaining the income of poor people has not been challenged. The 1986 Social Security Act, with its claim to be targeting the poor, in effect reaffirmed this principle, although in the process it discarded the 'national minimum'.

The 'rediscovery' of poverty in the 1950s (*Abel Smith and Townsend, 1960*) initiated, however, a concern over the definition of an adequate, minimum income which has refused to die. Since then numerous studies have argued convincingly that unemployment, low incomes and dependence on inadequate benefits have combined with other factors to increase the already large number of individuals living in poverty. For example, a survey of *Poverty and Labour* in London carried out by Townsend and his colleagues in 1985–6 revealed the widespread deprivation of families on low incomes and focused particularly on the problems faced by women, especially lone parents, and ethnic minorities. A broad spectrum of research encompassed in *The Growing Divide* demonstrated the polarisation of national living standards, with the gap between the top and bottom incomes of those in employment, and the quality of their health and housing, widening dramatically. CPAG's resume of current research *Poverty, the Facts* documented a growing catalogue of impoverishment amongst children, young people, elderly pensioners, and the homeless and, Bradshaw's study of living standards in Tyne and Wear has emphasised how difficult it is for families on benefit to maintain anything approaching a normal social existence. (*Townsend, 1987; Walker & Walker, 1987; CPAG, 1988; Bradshaw, 1989*).

In the Spring of 1989, the Secretary of State for Social Services, John Moore, was prepared to argue that poverty was a thing of the past and that current inequalities were the inevitable product of an increasingly affluent society (Speech to the Conservative Political Centre 11 May 1989). All the previous evidence belies his argument. The research already quoted has shown that in the 1980s the gap between the living standards of the poor and the rich has widened. Benefits have not, as Moore argued, improved in real terms so as to bring more below an ever more generous poverty line and people in receipt of benefits are frequently worse off than better off under the social security and housing benefit changes introduced by the 1986 Social Security Act. In addition, in the 1990s, the introduction of the community charge, popularly known as the poll tax, seems all set to shift even more resources to the rich from the poor (*Esam & Oppenheim, 1989*).

It is in this context that the role of local authorities in relation to the poor is crucial. Even within the changing legislative context, as major providers and organisers of services for education, housing, leisure, social services and welfare rights, local authorities are in a unique position to gain knowledge of the extent of poverty amongst their population and direct services to those in greatest need. As important local employers they are well-placed to encourage good employment practices especially in equal opportunities and low pay. As managers and planners they are closely involved with economic development, job creation training and transport and thus should be able to act on behalf of those areas particularly deprived. In their responsibility for environmental health and in their liaison with health authorities, concern over the relationship between inequalities and ill health can be turned into policy and effective practice. Similarly liaison with police and fire authorities can contribute to the development of 'safer cities' and in particular to the improvements of those deprived environments in which it is known that crime and accidents are concentrated. Thus local authorities can contribute in many ways to supporting the poor although it is undoubtedly central government with whom the final responsibility must rest.

There is, however, evidence to suggest that currently it is not the poor but the better off who benefit most from local authority services. A study of the pattern of expenditure of Cheshire County Council, for example, showed that heavy expenditure on items such as roads, parks, libraries, 16+ education and waste tips left the balance of expenditure in favour of those in the top income brackets though the poorest did receive greater benefit from pre-16 education and social services provision (*Bramley et al, 1989*). Evidence from the AMA's anti-poverty working group has also illustrated how nursery school places set up for children from poor families in inner city areas are taken up by those driven in from the more affluent suburbs and cheap leisure facilities are predominantly used by the middle classes. The effective targeting of local authority services is clearly no easy matter.

2. The AMA poverty survey

The AMA's earlier unemployment study had been limited to eight authorities selected as representative of particular regions and unemployment patterns but all AMA members were invited to participate in the new research into poverty. The steering group convened to guide this research (see Appendix 1) agreed that all interested authorities should have the chance to participate in what was seen as both a research and development exercise linked to future developments in local authority strategies. Fifty-two out of a possible sixty-nine member authorities agreed to participate, and forty-one ultimately responded to the survey launched in July 1987, with additional input from some fire and transport authorities (Appendix 2).

At an early stage in the research, pilot studies in the contrasting London Boroughs of Southwark and Richmond upon Thames illustrated how difficult this research would be to execute without the guiding hand of a local liaison officer. Accordingly such officers were nominated by authorities to facilitate the distribution of questionnaires and the collection of data. They formed a valuable network of information and advice which is still operational. Most liaison officers are located in policy units within chief executives' departments or in social services research units. The pilot studies also indicated the need for several different types of questions aimed not just at departmental activities or particular client groups but also at general issues such as access to services, economic development, decentralisation. The final substantial questionnaire was distributed to a maximum of ten departments in each participating authority.

The questionnaire sought information on the 'impact of poverty' on all local authority services including especially housing, education, personal social services, welfare rights, public health, safety, transport, employment, and recreation. The 'impact of poverty' had two dimensions, encompassing both the effects of poverty on local authority workloads and the response being made by local authorities to such effects. Evidence of increased workloads might prove of an anecdotal rather than statistical nature and be found in the increased use of certain services or the increased take-up of local authority administered allowances and benefits. Responses could also take many forms, ranging from a negative withdrawal of services to the positive development of centralised anti-poverty strategies; along this continuum initiatives developed by individual departments or special units might prove of importance. Such responses might emphasise maintaining and raising income levels, improving the take-up of benefits, facilitating access to services, rejuvenating the local labour market and targeting vulnerable groups or deprived areas. Parts I to IV of the questionnaire were concerned with all these issues.

Part V of the questionnaire focused rather differently on the activities of the particular departments or units concerned, i.e. education, environmental health, housing, social services, welfare rights, making allowance for the different composition of these in various authorities. This allowed the research to explore both levels of awareness and concern with poverty in different types of departments as well as to examine some of the boundaries and difficulties created by 'departmentalism' and attempts to overcome these by neo-corporatism.

Running through this research has been a consciousness of the significant interplay in poverty related issues between local authorities and other statutory and voluntary agencies. Here interest in the statutory sector has been related to health as poverty and ill health have been closely linked since the publication of the Black Report in 1980 (*ed. Townsend and Davidson, 1982*). Since then the former Health Educational Council's report, *The Health Divide* (*1987*), has shown a widening health gap between rich and poor with those at the bottom of the social scale having much higher death rates than those at the top. A report on *Deprivation and Ill Health* (*BMA, 1987*) has argued that poverty is sapping the health and talents of the unemployed and their families as well as exposing the elderly to extremes of cold, disability and loneliness. Colin Thunhurst's study of Sheffield has shown through a systematic inspection of mortality rates together with a set of census based indicators that mortality rates are consistently related to direct indicators of poverty (*Thunhurst, 1985*).

Public health is an issue on which local authority activity has changed substantially over the years. Recognition of the links between poverty and ill health, and the urgent focus on clean drinking water and adequate sewerage brought local authorities to prominence at the end of the nineteenth century, long before other service roles were developed. The growth of concern over public hygiene in the sale of food by shops and restaurants, the development of health education and concern for 'clean air' all extended local authorities' responsibilities. Yet public health, like poverty, ceased to be a pressing issue after Beveridge and was hard hit by the post-Seebohm reorganisation of social services. It suffered particularly from the transfer of community medicine to the health authorities in 1974. The local authorities' formal

5

responsibility was reduced and the health authorities did not seem to be very interested. Only recently has a renaissance of concern over public health taken place, signified by the publication of the Acheson Report. Concern for issues such as drug abuse, HIV Infection and AIDS, issues related to food and hygiene (salmonella, listeriosis) and pollution (e.g. legionnaire's disease) have once again emphasised the public health duties so well articulated before World War I. Increasing recognition of the complex links between poverty and ill health and the above issues is now fuelling the debate on the future directions in which those responsible for public health should be moving.

This survey also sought to go beyond the local authorities' own confines to look at relationships with voluntary organisations on poverty-related issues. Some anti-poverty strategies are now paying particular attention to these relationships, as the example of the London Borough of Southwark illustrates in Chapter Three. Relationships between local authorities, local industries and commercial interests were also regarded as crucial where poverty related issues were concerned. Part of this research therefore focused on the role that local authorities may play in economic development, job creation and training. One interesting aspect of this, discussed in Chapter Four, was to discover how an initial concern for reducing unemployment is being broadened into action to reduce deprivation on a wider scale, with economic development units working more closely than before with other local authority departments.

Given the broad perspective of this research, the return of the questionnaires from the forty-two authorities who finally participated by the spring of 1988 was regarded as satisfactory. Although some returns were incomplete, the majority provided such a wealth of information and additional documentation that their analysis has been both lengthy and complex. The following chapters present the key findings of this analysis and are supplemented by further information provided through an anti-poverty working group convened in June 1988 to explore the rapidly changing dimensions of anti-poverty strategy.

3. Conclusion

It should be stressed that this research had three important goals. Firstly, it sought to extend knowledge of the different poverty-related policies and practices pursued by local authorities and to make this knowledge more widely available. Secondly, through the research process itself, it aimed to encourage more local authorities to collect and analyse relevant information on a systematic basis and to explore the implications of this. Thirdly, it tried to develop guidelines for 'good practice', showing which policies and which methods for their implementation contributed more effectively to alleviating poverty. Out of this developed a fourth, more ambitious prospect – the development of coherent, corporate models for anti-poverty strategy.

These goals have been pursued in a period of rapid change in the relationships between central and local government. In fact it may be said that the changing context of local government activity since research commenced in 1987 has simultaneously made the research more significant and more difficult. Since then, local government has been put under increasing pressure to reduce expenditure and deliver services more efficiently. Such pressure has been codified in the legislation facilitating ratecapping, compulsory competitive tendering and the introduction of the community charge, i.e. the Rates Act, 1984, the Local Government Act, 1988, and the Local Government Finance Act, 1988. Further measures could add to this pressure, in particular a proposal to give the powers to fix charges for services, including those provided by social services departments, to the Secretary of State for the Environment. Such measures are likely to have a cumulative effect as restricted and changing patterns of local authority services are called on to respond to increasing levels of need.

II Finding Out About Poverty

1. Local poverty profiles

Before the main survey was launched, all AMA authorities were asked for definitions and measures of poverty either currently in use or being collected. A positive response revealed a wide range of content and style in the collection and use of poverty-related statistics; this was later confirmed and supplemented by Part Two of the survey. In the two ensuing years the use of such statistics has been extended and refined and an increasing number of authorities, including metropolitan boroughs and county and district councils are now in the process of initiating or developing 'poverty profiles'. The following illustrates how a selection of these authorities have set about collecting information on local patterns of deprivation.* It is essentially a generalised account for the lay reader and will undoubtedly leave statisticians dissatisfied!

An early attempt to measure poverty in a local authority was carried out in Lambeth in 1973 by consultants engaged by the Department of the Environment to work on the Lambeth inner area study. As a rudimentary poverty line, a guideline of supplementary benefit entitlement plus 20% was used with a 7% weighting for the cost of living in London. 29% of local households were then judged to be in poverty. Following this, policy officers collected information from a variety of sources but found the statistics difficult to co-ordinate '. . . it was impossible to relate, for example, the number of children receiving free school meals to gross figures of supplementary benefit claimants

---

* Poverty profiles mentioned in this chapter are listed alphabetically, according to local authority, at the end of the Bibliography (page 89).

or to the sole source of household incomes available at that time which was the Greater London Transport Survey of 1971'.

In 1985 a further attempt to identify the extent of poverty and deprivation in Lambeth was made using the Department of the Environment's much criticised national league table of deprivation and the GLC's ward index of deprivation. The former index is criticised because it distorts levels of deprivation by averaging them out across the large provincial cities and then comparing these with the individual and much smaller London boroughs, thus producing a ranking of deprived authorities that is rather misleading (Flynn, 1986). Two further useful sources emerged in the results of the 1981 Greater London Transportation Survey and DHSS data on supplementary benefit claimants. The deprivation, income and claimants data were then all distributed on a ward basis to which were added current figures of registered unemployment by ward. The report *Deprivation and Poverty in Lambeth* was the result. Subsequently a *Social Audit of Lambeth* was conducted by a firm of consultants to assess the impact of Government policy since 1979. Pressures on the authority prohibited the growth of a corporate anti-poverty strategy which could fully utilise this knowledge (*Hibbitt, unpublished, 1988*), but there is now further discussion of development of both the strategy and a comprehensive poverty profile.

Other authorities to become involved early on in the collection and systematic use of poverty-related statistics included Bradford, Southwark, Greenwich and Manchester. Bradford produced an impressively illustrated loose-leaf book entitled *Poverty, Health and Disadvantage* in 1987. This report comple-mented an earlier study *Bradford in Figures*, which provided simple statistics, and *District Trends* which had identified key issues facing Bradford. The document's aim was to 'identify the links between poverty, health and disadvantage and to build up an overall picture of what is happening in different parts of the district'. Ultimately this information was intended to provide a basis for decisions on how and where money was spent. This document was compiled by officers from both the council and health authorities and is therefore an unusual example of collaboration. Its contents are similar to those of the two separate documents produced in the same year by the London Borough of Southwark – *Fair Shares: The Southwark Poverty Profile* and *Southwark's Health*.

The 'area profiles' of Bradford and Southwark differ considerably in approach from those of Greenwich and of Manchester. Greenwich commissioned MORI to construct a *Breadline Greenwich* analysis based on the measures employed in the 1983 *Breadline Britain* national survey conducted by MORI for London Weekend Television (*Mack & Lansley, 1985*). This had focused on the necessities or essential items that a majority of people thought were part of an acceptable lifestyle and on those who could not afford these items. Apart from indicating a high level of relative poverty in Greenwich – 25% – *Breadline Greenwich* also produced evidence on attitudes to the poor, fuel poverty, health, personal difficulties, benefit recipients and attitudes among the people of Greenwich to public services. The MORI survey was carried out in 1983. Subsequently a social services survey has shown that population projections anticipate an increase in the number of people in groups vulnerable to poverty and a study of poverty and housing has pinpointed those 'areas of stress' where housing conditions are particularly poor. It had been hoped that subsequent studies might show what use the poorest in Greenwich were making of council services but this did not prove possible.

Manchester is another authority in which reports on poverty have been developed and refined in approach. In October 1986 Manchester published its second investigation into the nature and causes of poverty in the cities. The report *Poverty in Manchester* described a city in which 24% of the work-force was unemployed, 31% of residents dependent on supplementary benefit and 47% of school children receiving free school meals. The third investigation into poverty in Manchester, published at the end of 1988, sought like Greenwich to move beyond the traditional approach to measuring poverty which involved the concept of a poverty line based on the level of supplementary benefit. It recognised that this approach was flawed because supplementary benefit, now income support, is not a measure of minimum national income and is limited in its availability and take-up. As in Greenwich, therefore, Manchester's third investigation into poverty used the methods adopted in *Breadline Britain* and looked at the standard of living which people in Manchester were able to afford. It concluded that many Mancunians have a standard of living which falls below the minimum acceptable in our society today. The proportion of Manchester residents currently lacking necessities because they cannot afford them is in many cases higher than that found nationally in 1984. Again, using the national criteria established in 1984, it seems that today a third of Mancunians are in poverty and nearly one-fifth are in deeper poverty lacking five or more necessities. The survey also confirmed the now familiar categories of people most at risk of such poverty: households with at least one person unemployed, one parent families, black and Asian households, pensioners living alone, people with disabilities or longstanding health problems, council tenants and large families.

The findings of the third Manchester investigation have been supported in different ways by the almost simultaneous publication of poverty profiles for

Map 1: Liverpool – Overall Deprivation Index

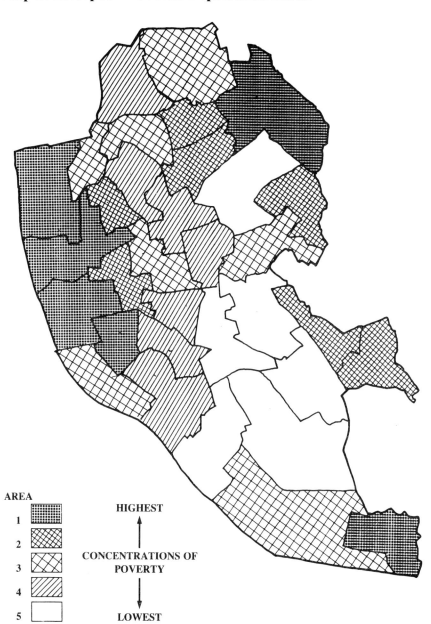

Source: 'Poverty in Liverpool', Liverpool City Council, December, 1988.

Birmingham, Lewisham and Liverpool. These studies all highlight the problems of decline in the inner city, showing that despite years of effort directed at combating inner city decline, problems such as poor housing, low pay, unemployment and racism are still prevalent and normally concentrated in a small number of very deprived areas. In Liverpool, for example, six out of thirty-three wards are described as severely deprived (see Map 1).

2. Developing a poverty profile

Apart from the *Breadline Britain* approach of Greenwich and of Manchester's third study, these profiles use census statistics supplemented by more up-to-date, local information. Indices based on the census to indicate deprivation by ward are widely used in most studies. Townsend's *Poverty and Labour in London* (*op cit*), useful for all London authorities, ranks all of London's 755 wards for multiple deprivation in terms of four indicators from the 1981 census – unemployment, overcrowding, not owning a car and not owning or buying a home. This provides a basis to which can be added further information on such factors as low income, housing, unemployment, education and health. Census material is also used as a basis for cluster analysis, whereby types of poverty in areas as small as enumeration districts can be identified. In Lewisham, for example, eight clusters were identified in different areas of the borough. Whilst based on dated information, the advantage of this method is that it allows individual estates or even streets with particular difficulties to be pinpointed. It also gives to councillors, local people and other interested parties a detailed breakdown of a particular area, which is useful in the planning of local services.

Adding up-to-date information to a poverty profile initially based on census statistics is difficult. National surveys and official statistics, apart from the census small area statistics, do not provide detailed, local information. Some official statistics, such as those for unemployment, have had their base line changed so many times that they have lost credibility (*Taylor, 1987*). Up-to-date information on particular groups of people, such as ethnic minorities, lone parents, or homeless families, may be altogether absent. Local authorities need, therefore, to expand their own, local research in order to compensate for this and develop a sound basis for effective decision-making and targeting. This need not automatically involve either original research or the expenditure of vast sums of money. Much information can be obtained from an authority's own records if these are maintained in a suitable and centralised form and are easily transferable from one department to another. Experience has shown however that, at the moment, much of local authority's record keeping is inadequate for its own research purposes and is rarely developed with this in mind. Health authorities, fire and police authorities, voluntary organisations, and local institutions of higher education may also provide rich sources of information if approached.

The rest of this chapter examines, therefore, how local authorities may set about the difficult task of assembling their own poverty related statistics. The general categories of low income, including unemployment and low pay, debt, housing, education, health, accidents and fires and vulnerable groups have been selected for this discussion, omitting for the moment the more controversial areas of social pathology, such as child abuse and crime, where the relationship with poverty is contentious, even though many think of it as self evident. (*For example, Blom Cooper, 1985.*)

I. Low income

There is without doubt inadequate information on low incomes on a small area basis. Official, published information from, for example, the *Family Expenditure Survey*, the *New Earnings Survey*, and the DSS's statistics on low income households, is not available for the local, ward level but only for a borough as a whole. Even the value of some of this is questionable. The DHSS for example used to provide statistics on the number of people receiving an income of 140% of supplementary benefit or less (*Low Income Families*) but this has now been discontinued and replaced by *Households Below Average Income*. Some feel this new series underestimates poverty levels quite seriously because it does not compare incomes with any external standard and glosses over inequalities of income between different members of a household (*Johnson and Webb, 1989*). DSS benefit records, available from the quarterly survey, are also on a borough basis while other records are for DSS areas which do not coincide with borough or ward boundaries. Lambeth, as mentioned, surmounted the problem of inadequate information by using income data for London and relating it to local characteristics in order to estimate income levels in the *Lambeth Social Audit* and Southwark utilised the responses to questions on income obtained by the *London Docklands Housing Needs Survey*, but such local solutions are not necessarily available for others.

Alternatively, local authorities can turn to their own information on housing benefit payments which can be accurately related to specific localities if, that is, collaboration between finance and housing departments can be ensured as housing benefit is administered by both. In Sheffield a recently published review of areas of poverty showed how the distribution of housing benefit claimants could be used to redefine the boundaries of areas of acute poverty more accurately. It is interesting, and possibly ironic, to note that new administrative arrangements currently in hand for registration and payment of the poll tax may lead to a co-ordination of benefit information on a borough wide basis which will then make it possible to locate those on low incomes very precisely.

The main causes of low income are unemployment, low pay and inadequate benefits. Unemployment statistics are problematic. For a start, since October 1979 official definitions of unemployment have been changed well over twenty times, making it difficult as said to record changes in the unemployment rate over time with real credibility. Local authorites may feel that unemployment in their own area has been under estimated. In London, the London Research Centre uses its own projections of the economically active population in the boroughs to provide what it regards as more realistic unemployment figures for local authority use. Another difficulty with unemployment information is that it does not give details of local ethnic minority unemployment. Authorities can work this out for themselves, as did Lambeth through its *Housing Needs Survey*. The importance of establishing this information was confirmed by a recent report from the Department of Employment which acknowledged that the national unemployment rate for black people was double that for whites. (*Department of Employment Gazette analysis of data from the Labour Force Survey, December 1988*). A further problem with unemployment statistics is that they under-represent female unemployment. For a variety of reasons many women unable to obtain employment do not register themselves as unemployed, frequently reverting to the identity of 'housewife' when employment becomes difficult or scarce and not seeking work when they feel there is little point. (*Martin and Roberts, 1984.*)

Along with unemployment, low pay has been identified as both a serious cause and indicator of persistent poverty. The link between the two is a strong one anyway, because high unemployment rates always exert downward pressure on wages. The Low Pay Unit's definition of low pay is based on the minimum pay level which is adequate without overtime and in 1989 stood at £143.66 per week (£3.78 per hour) for part-time workers which is two-thirds of male earnings. This is broadly similar to the Council of Europe's decency threshold of 68% of all adult full-time earnings – £148.51 (£3.91 an hour) for a 38 hour week. Using the *New Earnings Survey* it is possible for a local authority to calculate how many people are low paid, always allowing for the fact that the survey excludes both firms with below twenty employees and those not paying national insurance and so certainly underestimates the problem. It has been noted that, as employers themselves, local authorities have many low paid workers and that any investigation of low pay on their part might well have to lead to a different wages policy being adopted.

In Coventry the West Midlands Low Pay Unit recently completed a survey of low pay in the city which may be used as the basis for developing Coventry's anti-poverty strategy. The report concluded that low pay is a major contributor to poverty in Coventry, with 44.8% of the working population earning below the LPU threshold. Women, black workers, young people between the ages of 16 and 25 and people with disabilities are disproportionately affected. Although unemployment has fallen in Coventry, with the official total of the unemployed reduced by 5,484 between March 1988 and March 1989, the numbers of low paid workers in Coventry were found to have risen by 3,350 in roughly the same period. The report commented that 'The creed of jobs at any price has given those employers looking for cheap labour the chance to cash in.' (*Potter, 1989.*)

II. Debt

An increase in serious debt has become a worrying feature of the economy at all levels in recent years. It is especially pronounced amongst those on low incomes, where unemployment and the high cost of housing often leads to mortgage, rent and rates arrears and borrowing from extortionate money lenders or 'loan sharks', Birmingham's poverty profile, for example, illustrated how council tenants' rent arrears have escalated since the changes in housing benefit in March 1988 and are concentrated in the city's deprived inner and outer estate areas. Rate arrears have risen similarly. Fuel debts and the accompanying disconnections have also risen but information on these can only be used by a local authority where detailed, local information becomes available. Richard Berthoud has recently pointed out (*Berthoud, 1989*) that 'Statistics about the extent of debt are even more unsatisfactory than those about the use of credit. Almost all of the information is derived from the administrative procedures of particular types of creditor. There is no consistency of definition; the statistics tend to focus on the enforcement procedures rather than on the arrears themselves; there is hardly any information on the extent of overlap between the families in debt to different creditors.' An attempt on the part of local authorities to collect and standardise the presentation of such information would clearly be both positive and helpful in their attempts to locate and support the poor – the poll tax could act as a catalyst for this.

III. Housing

Those on low incomes experience a wide range of material and social deprivation in housing, education and health. The *AMA Greater London Housing Condition Survey* (*1987*) found that whilst unsatisfactory housing was difficult to define, households with the following characteristics were more likely than others to occupy homes in an unsatisfactory condition – low income households and households with few or no savings or unemployed heads resident in private sector property; households in private rented, particularly unfurnished, accommodation; households in the private sector resident more than twenty years; households with heads aged under twenty-five or over sixty-five years. Similarly a report on *Areas of Stress in Greenwich* (*1985*) showed how such information could be used to map housing deprivation in detail. Housing departments also collect and use information of inadequate housing indicated by the numbers of vacant properties and the levels of crime and vandalism on council estates and the requests made for transfer from such estates. Wigan's report on housing stress, for example, has made good use of such details. The ultimate data on housing deprivation is of course that on homelessness and on those living in temporary accommodation. The Audit Commission recently recorded that the number of homeless in temporary accommodation had reached a record 27,000 individuals and families, Shelter estimated 150,000 young people homeless nationally and Centrepoint found a doubling in the numbers of young people sleeping rough in London between 1987 and 1989. (*Randall, 1989.*) What is not known, however, as a recently attempted head count of those sleeping rough in London has demonstrated, is the number entirely homeless in our major cities. Such statistics should, however, properly be included in any city's poverty profile.

IV. Education

In education the most common, up-to-date statistic used until recently has been the percentage of children in a school or area receiving free school meals. Recent changes in legislation (restricting free meals to those families claiming income support) have rendered information on free school meals much less useful and it is now more limited as an indicator of deprivation. Information on free school meals is not necessarily available on a school basis. In the Lewisham study, for example, it was necessary to seek permission from all primary schools in the borough to use their individual figures on free school meals because figures collected by ILEA were only normally available on a borough-wide basis.

In the Lewisham study, as in several others, the information thus collected showed not only a steady rise in the numbers claiming free school meals in the first half of this decade but also showed that claimants were undoubtedly concentrated in those areas of the borough identified as deprived by other indicators. In Leeds, free school meals information has been combined with reading attainment scores to produce a ranking of all primary schools used to indicate which schools should be included in the primary needs programme. Similarly, ILEA has used an index of educational deprivation in which, in addition to the percentages of children receiving free school meals, factors recorded include children with varying degrees of language difficulties, the percentage of ethnic minority children in schools, the percentage of children from families with four or more children of statutory school age or younger, the percentage of children from one parent families and the percentage of pupil turnover in the school. Current information of this sort may be used to flesh out a basic poverty profile. In the Southwark study, for example, information from the *Educational Priority Index* was used to build up a picture of multiple deprivation at ward level.

V. Health

The Black Report (*op cit, Chapter One*) demonstrated at a national level the relationship between material and social deprivation and ill health. At the local level this has been confirmed also by the *Jarman Index*. A survey of GPs by Jarman and his colleagues for the local health authorities produced an index of deprivation based on GPs' perceptions of the effect of the social circumstances of their patients on their workload. Used locally this shows clearly that areas emerging as the most deprived have the greatest needs for primary health care (Map 2).

Several local studies have researched the relationship between poverty and health at a deeper level. Notable examples include Colin Thunhurst's study of *Poverty and Health in the City of Sheffield* and Peter Townsend's studies of Bristol and Manchester. These studies rely heavily on a measure called the Standard Mortality Ratio (SMR) which is calculated by comparing the actual death rate observed for a population with the death rate that would be expected if each group in that population were at the national average. An SMR above 100 therefore implies that people die younger than average whilst a score below 100 implies they survive longer than average. Whilst SMR can be distorted by a transient population and the presence of long stay institutions in areas, it is good enough to demonstrate clearly a link between deprivation and early death. Local authority wards identified as areas of deprivation usually show above average death rates for the population as a whole. Death rates for children in their first year of life are also widely used

Map 2: The 'Jarman' Index

Confirmation of the pattern of deprivation in Lewisham can be obtained by using the Jarman index. A national survey of 1 in 10 GPs by Jarman and his colleagues for the local health authorities identified ten social and demographic factors that the doctors considered problematic. These were: the proportion of people aged over 65; the proportion of people of pensionable age living alone; the proportion of young children under 5; one-parent families; unskilled workers; unemployment; lack of basic amenities; overcrowding; migration (change of address within the past year); and ethnic minorities. These variables were then weighted according to the doctors' perception of their relative importance. This produced a measure of GPs perceptions of the effect of the social circumstances of the population on their workload. In Lewisham, the Deptford wards (excluding Grinling Gibbons), Hither Green and Rushey Green have the most effect on GPs workload.

Measure of GPs' Perceptions of the Effect of the Social Circumstances of the Population on their Workload

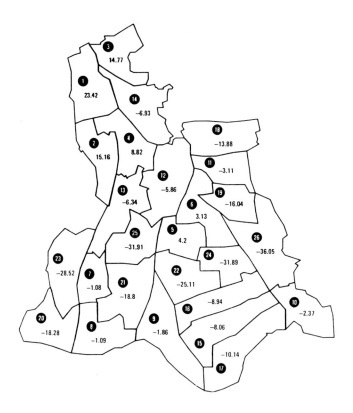

0 = average for Lewisham and North Southwark Health Authority

Source: Jarman. Reprinted from 'A Social Atlas of Poverty in Lewisham', Goldsmiths College, Centre for Inner City Studies, 1989.

as indicators of the social conditions and health of local communities; the two main rates in use are the infant mortality rate and the perinatal rate. The first measures the number of deaths of children aged less than one year who die in any particular year divided by the total number of live births, and the second measures the total number of still births plus deaths in the first week of life in any one year divided by the total number of births in that year. Thus the infant mortality rate looks at deaths in the first year of life and the perinatal mortality rate at deaths around child birth.

Information on mortality does not however tell us much about levels and patterns of illness and disability. Unfortunately, these are areas where local information is difficult to obtain. Problems exist for example because infectious diseases are often not reported and because hospitals from which statistics are compiled do not serve just local populations. The fact that the boundaries of local authorities and district health authorities do not coincide is yet another difficulty to be surmounted in obtaining information on local health.

VI. Accidents and fires

Where information can be obtained on the causes of death, accidents figure significantly amongst the younger age groups. *The Black Report* showed for example, that child pedestrian deaths have an extreme social class gradient and are concentrated in social classes four and five. It is not easy to prepare local information on this subject, as the Manchester study records, but where such information can be collected it is likely it will confirm that those most at risk of injury and death from accidents live in the most deprived areas. Several factors contribute to this such as living in an inner city area through which passes a large volume of traffic and not owning a car and thus being more at risk as a pedestrian. Much further information is needed on types of accidents and their relationship to deprivation both at home and in the work place but local and health authorities need to co-operate in the collection of this material. At the moment the report on *Road Accidents to Children in Manchester* prepared by a sub-group of the Black Report Working Party on Accidents to Children is almost unique.

Within the context of accidental death it seems relevant to introduce at this point information that became available through the *AMA Poverty Survey* on the location of domestic fires. One authority reported from a 1986 Fire Research Station Study that households experiencing fires had more contacts with social services departments than would generally be expected; larger households, those with several adults and children experience a higher fire incidence also. Fires were concentrated in relatively few enumeration districts and these appeared to be in the more deprived areas. Data from a wider study, for London and Birmingham, showed fire incidents to be correlated directly with family instability of which children in care is used as a 'proxy' or 'surrogate' measure. Other studies show illness or impairment to be a factor – 43% of victims of fire suffered from a physical or mental disability due either to illness or old-age. Impairment due to alcohol or drugs affected 16% of victims and most telling, 90% of the victims were in the lowest income groups including 39% who were pensioners or unemployed and 49% who were unskilled workers and their families (*Chandler et al*). Factors correlated by respondents to the AMA survey with fire incidents included proportions of owner occupation, low social and economic groups, unemployment and housing dissatisfaction. Again, as with health statistics, there is little readily available data collected by fire authorities on the relationship between fire and deprivation and this would seem to be an area in which statistics could probably be quite easily improved.

VII. Vulnerable groups

It is just as important to know 'who' are the poor as to establish where they live. Poverty profiles can usefully be extended by information on particularly vulnerable groups such as ethnic minorities, women, elderly people, single parents, people with disabilities, chronically sick and mentally ill people, carers, homeless people and others. In most cases available information is likely to be sketchy and dated and local surveys may be required. Good examples of these are Camden's recent survey on disabled people and Tameside's study of elderly black people. Effective targeting cannot be carried out without such information, as discussed in Chapter Five.

That such information is hard to come by is, however, an indication of the limited importance often attached to such groups. Women are a case in point. It is well known that, on average, in comparison with men, women receive less through earnings, benefits and pensions, have less command over resources and spend more time on unpaid work such as caring for children and dependent relatives and housework. Unfortunately, both national and local statistics mask women's poverty by using methods through which it cannot be easily identified. Both the 'consensus' approach typified by Mack and Lansley's *Poor Britain* and the measurement of household income, for example, fail to show that the distribution of resources within a family or household is often unequal, with women likely to be the losers (*Millar and Glendinning, 1989*).

Local authorities need therefore to develop new ways of identifying and measuring this poverty. Very much the same is true for ethnic minority monitoring, which needs to be extended in a sensitive but accurate manner.

3. Conclusion

This chapter has set out to demonstrate some of the methods through which local authorities may compile basic poverty profiles. It has also underlined some of the difficulties and pitfalls involved in trying to assemble information on deprivation on a local basis. In this activity local authorities can play an important part in the fight against poverty in compensating for inadequate official statistics and assembling information otherwise simply not available. Once prepared, a poverty profile may be put to use in a variety of ways. It may for example be used as a basis or a back up to an anti-poverty strategy. In the London Borough of Southwark, for example, the publication of both a poverty profile and a report on the health of the borough have been used to support work on anti-poverty policies. Profiles may also be used to advantage in creating an awareness of poverty related issues. They may form the focus for a conference such as was held, for example, in Southampton in July in 1988, or they may be used by Members of Parliament to create a national awareness of urban issues as has been the case with the third investigation of poverty in Manchester. Even where not employed effectively at the local authority level, poverty profiles may be put to good use by voluntary organisations and churches and other concerned bodies in the area in question. Their dual role, as factual documents of potential political influence as well as of local practical use, should not be underestimated.

Very recently, a European dimension has been added to poverty measurement. In Luxembourg the Eurostaats office is currently compiling league tables of European poverty and is producing poverty maps for EEC member countries. Poverty measurement is also becoming a key feature of funding proposals submitted by local authorities to the third European Community Action Programme. There are thus wider political and financial implications for poverty measurement than hitherto have been appreciated.

III Local Authorities and Anti-Poverty Strategies

1. Introduction

Local authorities have been developing their own perspectives on poverty since the late 1960s (*Berthoud et al, 1981*). Most have found that the difficulties of establishing and documenting a definition of poverty pale into insignificance against the problems of combating poverty. Nonetheless several have moved beyond individual, departmental initiatives towards the development of an 'anti-poverty strategy' – a corporate strategy whereby scarce resources can be more effectively directed towards poor people, services made more accessible to them and greater control over their own living standards made possible for them. Such corporatism looks beyond the organisational restructuring of the 1970s to focus more clearly on the needs of users and consumers. (*Stewart, 1983, Ch. 13.*)

Central government measures such as rate-capping, privatisation and the community charge (Chapter 1) have combined with other organisational and ideological difficulties to make the development and implementation of an anti-poverty strategy particularly difficult in the last two years. In the course of 1988, such strategies as existed became obviously and increasingly defensive under these pressures and some had to be abandoned. 1989 has, however, seen a resurgence of interest and support which, at the time of writing, appears to be gathering strength. There is no single explanation for this, but undoubtedly the effects of the implementation of the 1986 Social Security Act and subsequent changes including the funding of hostel provision, the rapid increase of homelessness and indebtness amongst poor people, and the efforts of the poverty lobby have served to heighten awareness of the severity of the current problems. These issues have all appeared on the agenda of many local authorities and have encouraged some councils to initiate new strategies.

This chapter attempts to review the characteristics and progress of some of the anti-poverty initiatives which have been developed since the mid 1980s, looking first at some of the London boroughs and then at a selection of other metropolitan authorities. Not all initiatives, by any means, can be included, and those which are described are not the only examples of interesting and imaginative practice. Their strengths, weaknesses and particular emphases do, however, serve to illustrate the type of conceptual thinking about poverty which has developed in the 1980s and some of the organisational responses which are occurring. What emerges quite clearly is that whilst anti-poverty strategies have much in common in their ideological approach to poverty, in organisational terms there is no 'blue-print' for local action. This account is deliberately descriptive in order to convey a sense of the content and direction which anti-poverty strategies are assuming.

2. Anti-poverty strategies in London boroughs

Several London boroughs embarked on anti-poverty activities in 1986 in the hope that 1987 would see a more sympathetic response from central government following the general election. In **Camden** an officers' meeting on 2 September 1986 welcomed the proposals for developing an anti-poverty strategy and agreed to set up four officer working groups to focus on income maintenance, fuel poverty, the council's charging policy and its debt recovery policies. These four issues remain at the forefront of all anti-poverty programmes. Camden recognised, however, that these were not the only key issues with employment/unemployment being a major omission. It was also agreed that officers working on the anti-poverty strategy proposals should link in with other council initiatives, e.g. regeneration, homelessness and health for all. The brief for each of the working group was:

(a) To find out what each department does.
(b) To look at what improvements could be made to existing services.
(c) To consider what initiatives could be taken.
(d) To consider the needs of the priority groups as set out in the council's manifesto.

Chief officers nominated officers to represent their departments on the working groups but not all departments were represented and this hindered early progress and was reflected in the piecemeal and sometimes inaccurate nature of information obtained. However, the general format looked promising and there were high hopes of its working. Information obtained from the various departments was collated in a common form based on a series of questions and this was followed by recommendations for improved action. Camden's programme was brought to a halt in 1987 as ratecapping and the closure of council posts began to take its effect. The Welfare Rights Unit still argues, however, that the council should have regard to its anti-poverty strategy in adopting policies (e.g. relating to charging, debt recovery and collection of the community charge on a weekly basis) which affect the poorest and most vulnerable sections of the community.

In **Lewisham** an informal anti-poverty working party (of councillors, officers and representatives of voluntary groups) met between August 1986 and February 1987. In this time the working party undertook a considerable amount of work which included drafting a council-wide anti-poverty strategy, reviewing key council services such as housing benefit, welfare rights and consumer services, and voluntary sector advice and information services. The working party obtained additional council resources for welfare rights, consumer services, money advice and for a research project to investigate the levels and patterns of poverty in the borough. Once funding had been agreed the working party disbanded, recommending that the council establish a formal member-level body to oversee the implementation and development of a council-wide anti-poverty strategy. In the event, such a body was never established, because of the considerable budget reductions which the council had to make. The central resources needed to support a corporate initiative were no longer available. The subsequent lack of central co-ordination resulted in a lower overall profile for anti-poverty work, although progress has been made within some service areas. The publication of the Goldsmiths research project (*Hyde et al, 1989*) at the beginning of 1989 helped to put anti-poverty back on the corporate council agenda. Chief officers were charged with developing proposals in response to the research findings. The Lewisham experience highlights therefore the usefulness of a local survey to bring the issue of poverty to the fore and to demonstrate the need for a council-wide approach. Without staff resources to co-ordinate, however, progress is likely to be uneven.

Four other London boroughs which commenced their work in anti-poverty in the mid 1980s have had better fortune in sustaining it. In **Greenwich** the policy and resources committee first set up an anti-poverty sub-committee in January 1987. This is serviced by an interdepartmental working party with the lead taken by the principal welfare rights officer. Like Islington and Southwark, this has no budget of its own but relies on existing departmental budgets to implement policy. Increasingly in Greenwich the need to raise fees and charges and reduce service provision has made the implementation of strategy more difficult, but this has not halted the effort to raise departmental awareness of poverty-related issues. Progress has been made particularly in the general field of debt collection: the housing department has reviewed its rent collection procedures to take greater account of poverty and the rates department have developed special guidelines on section 53 of the General Rating Act 1957 and regularly distribute specially prepared leaflets for those on low incomes. A paper on corporate debt recovery policy has been prepared to draw such practices into a coherent strategy. Further, agreement has been reached on repayment rates for the imminent poll tax allowing those on low incomes to pay both by fortnightly instalments and by giro. Two further recent developments are also of significance: firstly, approval has been obtained for the setting up of an independent, specialist money advice service in the borough; secondly, a proposal is being considered in council to set up a new benefits unit within the chief executive's department to unify poll tax rebates with housing and educational benefits and to develop welfare rights work further. All these developments underline the extent to which Greenwich Council has raised the awareness of the problems of those on low incomes and is now developing strategies which take account of these.

Hackney Council adopted an anti-poverty strategy in 1986 but its proposals could never be fully implemented as the necessary growth and organisational change involved became increasingly unrealistic in the financial climate prevailing then. Facing up to those realities the policy and resources committee resolved in December 1988 to pursue an anti-poverty strategy specifically tailored to take account of the social and financial climates to be faced. It was agreed that the strategy should be advanced on a small number of selected fronts with the most important priority being to scrutinise the ways in which the council's decision-making has an impact on the poorest, most vulnerable and disadvantaged groups in Hackney.

A first step was the establishment of an anti-poverty management team (APMT) consisting of a small core group of officers to provide a corporate overview, and representatives from specific service areas. The APMT is chaired by the director of social services and the director of environmental health and consumer protection. It meets monthly to identify the anti-poverty implications of the council's programme. Its first task is to identify which committee reports should include anti-poverty implications and to produce guidelines for officers on how to address anti-poverty implications in key areas. In addition the APMT will scrutinise key areas of the council's work programme and head officers working on areas such as rent arrears and the Section 1 budget will be asked to attend the APMT to present their proposals for scrutiny. In the case of the poll tax, the APMT will be represented on the poll tax steering group and that representative will ensure that anti-poverty implications are built into any proposals. The strategy is seen as an integral part of the council's equal opportunities policies and seeks to redress disadvantage and discrimination particularly on behalf of black people, people from ethnic minorities, women and people with disabilities.

Although no direct expenditure is required to implement this anti-poverty strategy, it is dependent on a small number of staff being released from their normal duties to participate in the group each month. In fact the work of the APMT is seen as cost-effective in the long term. Its first report argues that 'there is a real danger that decisions taken now which do not consider the long-term impact on local people will lead to greater expenditure in the long run. This will be particularly acute where decisions in one area do not take account of impact on another statutory service'.

In **Islington**, the policy review group, chaired by the leader, gave top-level endorsement for an anti-poverty strategy in 1986. A cross-departmental team was set up to oversee the development of this, drawing from varying levels of officer and organised by the welfare rights co-ordinator, seconded to this work on a more or less full-time basis. Working groups were set up on the Social Security Act, fuel poverty, housing issues, debt recovery, disability, ethnic minorities, employment and low wages and social services related issues, but for various reasons the last three never got off the ground. The omission of groups concerned with economic development and women was recognised: the first was an economy as the council already had an economic development unit with modest resources and clearly established priorities; the second was left out because it made sense for issues affecting women to be integrated into the rest of the strategy with the support of the women's units.

Each of these issue-based working groups was given the same brief to use as a reference point in its activities. This suggested that groups should seek to:

1. Assemble relevant research and policy
2. Survey relevant services
3. Evaluate the impact on poverty of services and their relation to the objectives of the strategy
4. Identify specific proposals to improve policies and service delivery

5. Prioritise according to existing resources
6. Seek alternative or council funding
7. Consider factors affecting the broader context, such as Social Security laws, fuel boards' policies, etc.

The work of the debt recovery group provides a good illustration of how Islington's strategy is working. The membership of this group is drawn from housing, finance, legal and social services departments, a neighbourhood officer from the chief executive's department, a trading standards officer, a financial adviser on improvement grants, welfare rights workers and staff from the Citizens' Advice Bureaux and law centres. The group's first act was to survey the areas of debt recovery for which chief officers are responsible. This was followed by the adoption of the general debt recovery policy recommended in the joint report of the National Consumer Council (*Consumers and Debt, 1983*). Because of the concern with increasing indebtedness it was agreed to take measures to encourage the development of credit unions and to plan and seek funding for a money advice centre to respond to the growing incidence of multiple debt and the increased activity of loan sharks. This led to a number of recommendations, some of which have already been implemented. These included the re-design and re-writing of information sent to ratepayers, earlier information on seeking advice, information in ethnic minority languages, basic training in money advice skills for rate recovery officers, the use of discretionary 'write off' powers in cases of hardship, better communication between rates and housing benefits sections where a debt is increasing and anticipation of the community charge's implications. The continuing need for a strategy is confirmed by the emergence of new issues arising from legislation and the financial pressures on the council, creating new needs for a balance between economic imperatives and an anti-poverty strategy. The latter's credibility has been re-affirmed and it looks all set for another year of activity.

The development of a formal anti-poverty strategy in **Southwark** properly began with the establishment of the anti-poverty strategy team (APST) in 1986. At its first meeting in January 1987 this co-opted representatives from all departments and made the director of public protection services the lead officer. Later that year the initiative was supported by the publication of the poverty and health profiles previously mentioned. A joint council/churches conference on *Faith in the City* then led to the setting up of a joint anti-poverty commission, chaired by the director of public protection and aiming to develop inter-sector collaboration on anti-poverty work. A council health sub-committee to pursue the implementation of health and poverty profiles was also established.

A lack of commitment from departments in the face of increasing constraints on services resulted in the termination of the APST in February 1988. However, the adoption by the policy committee of the results of the health and poverty profiles as base material in service delivery planning and as a major element in a new council-wide system for the prioritisation of capital projects, saved the strategy from collapse. This illustrates how valuable sound research can prove to be. Most recently (April 1989) a *Healthy Southwark* group has been set up leading to the adoption of a partnership approach to anti-poverty work for the future. This group contains representatives from council, health authorities, churches, voluntary and community groups and businesses. The object is to develop a comprehensive joint strategy to improve the quality of life of people living and working in Southwark. Three main themes are action on health, poverty and the environment.

The move away from an anti-poverty strategy based primarily on action within the council towards more collaborative work with other agencies and members of the community is a result of a variety of factors. Clearly, the fact that as the council has faced ever more severe financial and staff shortages, departments have not felt able to commit scarce resources to planning activities rather than service delivery has made corporate co-ordination more difficult. Hence the demise of the APST. It is considered, however, that the APST achieved as much as was practicable. It ensured that up to date, comprehensive information is available to serve as a basis of all future service planning. Arrangements have been made to update this as necessary. Achieving political acceptance of poverty and health as prime determinants of the future direction of Council policy and priorities will ensure that responsibility will now rest with staff in each department to ensure that these issues are fully considered in developing future plans – good examples of the way in which this has been done are the recently produced *Housing Strategy* and the *Education Development Plan*. In these circumstances it is not felt that there is a continuing need for a corporate mechanism: anti-poverty initiatives are the province of all staff.

Perhaps more important, however, is the view formed very early on that poverty is about much more than lack of material resources, but is concerned with questions of social justice and inequality over which the council alone has little influence. Fundamental to Southwark's approach, therefore has been a desire to work with the community – empowering people to articulate their own needs and to find local solutions to many of the problems of isolation. The basis of Southwark's strategy now, therefore, is to build partnerships with other agencies (statutory and voluntary) and with the community to develop a wide range of local projects. These include a child accident prevention project, the development of credit unions, action to enable voluntary groups to find premises more easily, the establishment of a tools library, the designation of an anti-poverty partnership where community self-help and advocacy will be promoted as a means of targeting services and resources. While it is too early yet to say how successful this approach will be, there are signs that the people in the borough are keen to be involved, and that there is scope for the development of much closer links with other agencies.

The experiences of these four London boroughs reveals how differently similar objectives and policies may be translated into practice. Greenwich has developed the role of its cross-departmental working party, Hackney has focused on the implications of its council's decisions, Islington has expanded the activities of its issue based working groups and Southwark has moved its base of operations much closer to its communities. Each approach has been a response to the exigencies and difficulties encountered in the early stages of its anti-poverty strategy and shows that, for a strategy to survive, it must be prepared to be flexible and imaginative and responsive to changing circumstances.

In many respects the progress towards corporate anti-poverty strategies has been more pronounced outside London than within the London boroughs. The differences of scale between large metropolitan authorities and the much smaller London boroughs do however make comparisons somewhat suspect, even when the principles at issue are the same. The following selective accounts of anti-poverty strategies serve to illustrate the directions in which a number of authorities are now travelling. Of necessity, these accounts are neither exclusive nor fully comprehensive.

3. The North West

In **Manchester** an anti-poverty sub-committee was set up in 1985 to develop a council-wide strategy. When the second *Poverty in Manchester* report was published in 1986 it was circulated to all departments who were then asked to provide information on how they were trying to respond to the report's findings. These responses formed the basis for the policies which were formalised into a statement of principles for an anti-poverty strategy in September 1987 and from which has come the latest statement of principles in Manchester's third investigation into poverty.

These principles, against which the council's services are to be examined include:

- ensuring as far as possible that an individual's level of income does not affect their ability to participate in decisions about issues which affect them;
- the provision of services on the basis of need rather than income;
- the collection of outstanding debts and charges in as sensitive a manner as possible to ensure that further hardship, distress or financial difficulties are not created;
- the maximisation of individual income levels wherever possible, especially for those dependent on benefits, and the low waged, through comprehensive provision of information and advice, and the prompt, sensitive and accurate administration of benefits;
- a programme of education and information aimed at raising the level of awareness amongst the public at large, individuals, groups and communities, about the extent of poverty, its origins and effects and possible remedies;
- providing skills, training, and encouragement to those in need, in order to enable them to speak for themselves, and to overcome their experiences of dependency and powerlessness;
- ensuring that the benefits arising from capital investment and revenue expenditure by the council accrue to those in greatest need.

Between October and December 1987 Manchester was involved in a massive restructuring which deducted £110 million from the council's budget. Frontline services were protected where possible, including those particularly concerned with poverty, such as the Manchester Benefits Service. In this difficult situation the pressure has been on departments to implement the 1987 principles. All seventeen departments have been asked to submit action plans to the AP sub-committee; eight have so far responded with very interesting reports from engineers and planning – departments that are not necessarily associated immediately with anti-poverty.

In Manchester there is a strong feeling that the political will behind this activity has grown since the start of 1989. However, staff resources have not been allocated centrally to pursue the work faster. This is regarded as necessary in order to develop approaches to policies and practice across the organisation.

Currently Manchester is working to improve its anti-poverty strategy in three key areas: information – how best to update and disseminate poverty related statistics; the council's role as an employer – how to raise the level of pay of lower-paid council employees and link anti-poverty strategy to equal opportunities policies; how to improve the council's role as a service provider. From these efforts it is hoped that eventually a full, corporate anti-poverty strategy will arise. The council will then be able to make a public declaration on poverty and make its stand against poverty more widely known.

In **Bolton** poverty was introduced as a major area of concern into the council's strategy statement in November 1987. Since then a poverty review group has been established consisting of a representative of each department and chaired by the assistant chief executive. In its first review the group made two major decisions: the first was to concentrate on financial poverty, although fully recognising the wider causes of hardship and the importance of a relative definition of poverty going beyond that of low income; the second was not to pursue any further facts and figures on poverty but to concentrate on policies for relieving that poverty that is already widely perceived in Bolton. In these two respects Bolton's approach differs considerably from that of Manchester.

Drawing on the experiences of AMA members, Bolton looked for strategies which could help poor people maximise their incomes. It found that Bolton provided relatively little welfare rights advice direct to the public and lent support to the establishment of a benefits working group which brings together operational staff involved in take-up campaigns, training and benefits administration in order to develop a co-ordinated and corporate approach to these aspects of anti-poverty work. The review group 'has no doubt that a wider authority of advice to local residents, coupled with effective public awareness campaigns, would have an immediate and wide-ranging benefit. It is the most effective course of action that the council could take in the short-term to address the problem of poverty.' (*Report of the Poverty Review Group, 13.1.89*). It was subsequently decided to adopt a strategy which would involve a wide range of the council's front line staff in giving simple and straightforward advice, backed up by a specialist team of whom more complex cases could be referred. This would provide a better fit with the type of advice most needed, involve many staff in this priority area and assume a positive approach that assisted clients in the context of other services rather than reacting to requests on welfare rights alone. It would also make the most effective use of specialists skills. This strategy needs an emphasis on high quality training and support for council staff, which the specialist unit will provide. One significant benefit of this strategy is that an appropriate level of training could easily be extended to other people, for example from the voluntary sector. The review group believes such an extension would increase the impact in the borough particularly if the specialist referral service were also available to such people. It would also develop a partnership approach with the voluntary sector. Finally, of course, training would be available for any members who would find it helpful.

The group has also looked at ways of assisting individuals with indebtedness. Apart from developing the partnership approach through the funding of an additional debt counsellor at the Bolton Citizen's Advice Bureau in return for basic debt counselling training for the authority's staff, it is also examining the possibility of encouraging the establishment of credit unions in Bolton. It is also searching, as are many authorities, for ways of improving its own debt recovery procedures. Dealing with debtors in Bolton is done in accordance with a code of practice. Here the emphasis is on contacting defaulters as early as possible and not allowing debts to linger and accumulate. Not only does the code insist on dealing with people face to face, but it also requires an approach to them that is friendly and receptive and not frightening. Letters are couched in simple language and Acts, section of Acts etc. are deliberately not quoted. Letters are regularly monitored for clarity and friendliness. The Bolton 'softly softly' approach works well. With a mortgage portfolio of £3m, debts have been reduced to £70,000. The rates debt which in 1986 stood at 2.9% of all rates payable had been reduced to 1.7% by 1988 with in effect a reduction of 50%. Much of this has been achieved by talking to individuals in arrears and accepting realistic payments that they could afford rather than taking them to court. The punitive approach is seen as counter-productive, particularly when it leads to families becoming homeless and thus creating financial and social burdens for the authority itself.

The Bolton approach requires an emphasis in staff training on using the telephone in a friendly way and on interviewing and listening to clients sympathetically. Whilst this may seem tantamount to 'common sense' it is in fact based on a belief in the willingness of the client to pay as and when able. This belief is not widely shared by local authority officers nor by the public and many believe that defaulters simply refuse to pay their debts. A straightforward piece of research, taking a sample of those in rates or mortgage arrears off a local authority register, could be used to settle this argument and provide a firmer basis for debt recovery policy. It should be pointed out that neither credit unions nor more persuasive debt recovery procedures directly tackle the causes of poverty and, in particular, the problems created by unemployment and low pay. This does not, however, negate the value of the methods discussed nor preclude pursuing strategies aimed specifically at reducing unemployment and raising pay levels.

In addition to maximising benefit take-up and assisting those in debt, the poverty review group is also concerned to investigate the council's concessionary charging policies, looking in particular at a more unified approach to the marketing of council concessions (for individuals) across council services to include the leisure visa scheme, education concessions, library services and so forth and at a method for determining the eligibility for concessions within a more corporate framework.

In **Kirklees**, as in Bolton, it was felt that a poverty profile would not add much to the knowledge already available in the council of widespread poverty. What was needed was action and having received the political commitment to this the poverty action working group was set up in July 1987. This group was a partnership between voluntary sector representatives and local authority officers. Its open door philosophy meant that anyone from an organisation with a genuine concern with poverty issues could attend meetings and join in with the work of the various groups. It was organised into a plenary group and a number of different sub-groups concerned with unemployment, education and training, community enterprise, health promotion benefits publicity, childcare, the elderly and debt. Reports from these groups were used to define specific proposals for action. This working group has now been superseded by the poverty task force which is a higher profile working group through both elected members and officers. It is currently discussing the representation of the voluntary sector.

The council's strategy is backed up by a £40,000 pool for use as seed corn money to initiate small projects. On a grander scale is the 'Engine for Growth' company in which both council and local businesses work together to stimulate social and economic regeneration, linking profitable schemes with projects with a social bias. Recently, in this context, Kirklees has announced a £200m joint venture with Henry Boots of Sheffield to build a major shopping scheme in Huddersfield to be followed by numerous smaller developments throughout Kirklees. This element in Kirklees anti-poverty strategy is an exciting one which is breaking new ground in the nature of the collaboration between the local authority and private enterprise.

Recently the Institute of Local Government Studies at Birmingham University was commissioned by Kirklees Council to review the council's committee structures and processes. Whilst reducing the number of sub-committees, INLOGOV recommended two new, absolutely key sub-committees – the community and economic regeneration sub-committees of policy and resources. These do not have delegated powers of their own and were originally designed to co-ordinate and work through a group of service committees as follows:

- Economic regeneration sub-committee: to work through environment, highways, planning and economic development.
- Community regeneration sub-committee: to work through education, housing, leisure services and social services.

Working procedures have however shown that this division of labour is unrealistic and now each sub-committee has a remit to work across the whole council. All this indicates the type of rethinking of local government structures that may take place when a concern for economic and social regeneration is placed at the top of a council's priorities. Authorities embarking on the development of a corporate anti-poverty strategy would do well to take note!

4. The North East

The two authorities considered within this category provide further interesting examples of developments that have gathered speed since the 1987–8 AMA survey. Both Newcastle and North Tyneside have had initiatives to combat poverty since the mid 1970s but the persistence and worsening of deprivation in the 1980s, coupled with changes in the role of local authorities as debt collectors, have caused them to review policies and to move closer to the establishment of a corporate anti-poverty strategy.

Newcastle has been making a special effort to challenge the causes and effects of poverty since the late '70s when it established its economic development committee, (which now has a revenue budget of £2.4m) and set up the priority areas project. The latter has sought to attack stress and improve conditions in the inner city's priority wards through the efforts of 14 priority area teams. Each team is made up of three ward councillors and a full-time officer of the PAT project, has a budget of £40,000 to spend on projects to benefit local residents and encourages local community action. Since their creation, however, the PATs have regularly expressed feelings of marginalisation and recently this has contributed to the growing conviction in Newcastle that the attack on poverty should be strengthened corporately.

The development of Newcastle's anti-poverty strategy stems also from evidence of intensive and worsening poverty in the city and from the fact that recent legislation means that local authorities will become more involved in debt collection than ever before. Over the last fifteen years there have been sharp increases in Newcastle in the numbers of three social groups who are known to be especially vulnerable to poverty – the unemployed, single parent families and the elderly. Others, such as ethnic minorities and certain groups of women, are also thought to be more at risk although their poverty is not so well documented. The authority is concerned that amongst such groups of people it will become more directly involved in debt collection as a result of changes in social security, housing and rates legislation. This new role is said to be most sharply felt by the housing department where the changes in housing benefit have proved so difficult to implement that arrears of over £1 million built up in the first six months of the operation of the revised system.

A corporate approach to poverty in Newcastle is likely to include three strands of anti-poverty strategy currently not prioritised. These include a focus on the local authority's role as an employer and the danger inherent in this of actually perpetuating poverty, a concern with inter-departmental working and ensuring that anti-poverty strategy does not become marginalised within one department (i.e. social services) or in the PATs and, thirdly, a focus on the involvement of the voluntary sector and the trade unions in all planning work.

As part of its anti-poverty strategy, Newcastle is keen to progress decentralisation. The housing department has already decentralised many of its functions to neighbourhood offices in order to improve local people's access to its services. Other community initiatives, such as the Cowgate Neighbourhood Centre (a health and social services-funded community social work project) have been effective in enhancing self-esteem and confidence. Participating in the management committee and the running of such centres enables local people to feel more in control of their lives and to tackle the powerlessness with which poverty is strongly associated. The anti-poverty strategy group is currently exploring the possibilities of a 'one-stop shop', whereby people can get access to a range of council services at only one delivery point. (*See Chapter Four.*)

In the last twelve months in Newcastle an officer working group and a member group on anti-poverty strategy have been meeting regularly. The first sub-group has been set up on 'charges'. The member group has called for 'budget impact statements' from service departments and also requested an analysis of poverty indicators by enumeration districts based on the 1981 census. A report has also been presented on the extent of poverty in areas of the city outside what would normally be considered the priority areas. Officers are now planning a conference on poverty and young adults at which an update of the 1984 Social Audit report will be launched.

In **North Tyneside** in 1989 poverty is estimated to be a fact of life for 30% of the population. The areas of Riverside, Chirton, Howdon, Longbenton and, for young people, Central Whitley Bay are known to be specially deprived. In the current development of a strategy for these areas and for groups of poor people throughout the borough, special anti-poverty measures are seen as less important than rethinking existing patterns and styles of operation. The council has stated 'An anti-poverty strategy is not a new area of policy or provision that can be devised and implemented in isolation. It is an approach which must underlie a major part of the council's services and be accorded a high measure of priority on a consistent and long-term basis.' Policies are being developed, therefore, on income support, charging, debts and arrears, low pay, economic development, housing and health issues, and community and childcare, which are applicable across departments. The economic development sub-committee is taking the lead in policy development. As yet there have been no administrative or budgetary changes to support the emerging strategy but these are in the pipeline along with the restructuring of all of the central services departments of the council.

One innovative step taken by North Tyneside has been the preparation of a *Happy Families* video and training pack. The video, set against the benefit changes in April 1988, follows the slide into debt of a typical family and the lack of choices open to it when faced with crisis, whilst the training pack contains practical information about the nature of poverty in Britain and considers positive action which can be taken by local authorities and community groups, for example in the development of housing co-operatives, food co-operatives and credit unions.

Other innovative steps have been the changing of the welfare rights service into an advice and information service which co-ordinates advice and information given both within the authority and with the voluntary sector across the borough; the setting up of an unemployment service unit, and a series of *Peoples Centres* run by the community in a structure which mirrors the provision of the advice and information network; the creation within the advice and information service of a team of credit union development workers to set up and support credit unions particularly in areas with a high incidence of deprivation; the development of social services family centres, creche provision linked to peoples centres and community high schools; after school care schemes and student child care schemes. A major conference on community participation in the anti-poverty strategy held in November 1989 aimed at community activists and was organised by members of management committees of local advice centres, tenants' groups, credit unions and other members of the voluntary sector. The conference was supported and funded by the council.

5. The West Midlands

Although there have been many poverty related initiatives throughout the West Midlands, which were well documented in response to the AMA survey, the development of centrally based anti-poverty strategy was less pronounced than in other areas of the country up to 1988. Recently however, in **Birmingham** an officers' anti-poverty strategy co-ordinating group has met for the first time and this has been followed by the publication in April 1989 of a very detailed poverty profile. The Birmingham group is large, consisting of over fourteen officers from a wide range of departments. Drawing on Islington's experience, it is considering setting up sub-groups to deal with particular areas in depth – in particular unemployment and low wages, debt and related issues, benefits and charging policies, health and poverty, fuel poverty, housing and environment. Initially each sub-group will be co-ordinated by a member of the anti-poverty co-ordinating group.

The officers' group reports to a newly established anti-poverty sub-committee of the finance and management sub-committee. The establishment of this new sub-committee was indicative of the growing commitment to deal with issues relating to poverty on a corporate basis.

6. Common characteristics and difficulties of anti-poverty strategies

The previous accounts illustrate that an anti-poverty strategy is most likely to be run by a committee based either within chief executive's, or possibly in a welfare rights unit or economic development unit, on which most key departments are represented. The function of the committee will be firstly to ensure that 'poverty' is considered in each department when policies are developed and resources deployed, secondly to ensure that each department targets the poorest groups of people and the poorest areas, thirdly to create a greater awareness of poverty among staff and fourthly to encourage joint action with the voluntary sector and other statutory bodies to relieve poverty.

Such a strategy may be set up without any additional budget. One of its prime purposes will then be the redirection of existing funds to those in greatest need. However, there is a feeling that budgetary issues are more complex than this suggests and that additional funding may be essential for anti-poverty measures to succeed. In a period of financial stringency and rate-capping this poses severe problems for some authorities. Finance directors and those controlling departmental budgets are key figures in the implementation of strategy, but the significance of their position is sometimes overlooked and overall patterns of budgeting are neglected.

The previous case studies, supplemented by information from the AMA's working group on anti-poverty strategy, also show that common problems arise where an anti-poverty strategy has been implemented. It has been found, for example, that the extent to which a poverty sub-committee can affect the working of an entire department is limited and piecemeal, especially in rate-capped boroughs where prior concern has been given to reducing expenditure. Procedures can quickly become bureaucratised and result in little or no action. Where one department institutes an economy measure, it may do so without due regard for the effect of this on other departments working with hard pressed clients e.g. a reduction in clothing grants by an education department or heating allowances from housing may end up being reflected in rising Section One payments in social services. Somehow departments have to be encouraged to work together, both for the good of their clients and for the overall efficiency of their authority.

Beyond these general difficulties, there are a number of more specific problems which may cause an anti-poverty strategy to falter or actually fail:

(1) An anti-poverty strategy may be restricted to one part of an authority with which it becomes so closely identified that expansion into the rest of the authority becomes difficult. Newcastle, for example, feels that its group of area priority teams, set up in 1976, and one of the first anti-poverty measures of its kind, is a case in point. Dissatisfaction with these teams has centred on their inability to influence the rest of the authority on, for example, health aspects or the collection of rates. A similar type of problem may arise should a strategy be set up within a welfare rights unit from which only a certain, limited perspective may be obtained. Obviously it is vital for an anti-poverty strategy to have an impact on all local authority activities including especially housing, education, health, transport, economic development and planning and personal social services.

(2) Serious failure may result from ignoring the importance of front line workers in both the local authority itself and local voluntary organisations. (As most front line workers are women, and most managers are men, one has to wonder if an element of sexual discrimination is at work in this case?) Recognising the valuable information held by front lineworkers, home helps, community workers, teachers, CABX staff, is important and some authorities are now making a major effort to involve the voluntary organisations in their strategy, for instance Islington, Kirklees and Southwark.

(3) Failure may also result from not recognising that social and economic

regeneration must proceed hand in hand. Economic advance may result, for example, as in London's Docklands, in more jobs for outsiders but few for the local residents with little improvement in housing or environmental facilities. (See Chapter Four) Social regeneration through community development will not succeed either if widespread unemployment persists. Therefore economic development and schemes for improving the quality of social life must not be viewed in isolation from each other.

(4) Where there is no general awareness of poverty as a significant issue, little progress will be achieved. To this end poverty reports, seminars and public meetings must be used to stimulate consciousness of poverty-related issues, particularly in those better off areas where poverty and the equal opportunities issues which accompany it can be so easily ignored. Again, co-operation between a local authority and its local voluntary groups is vital.

(5) An anti-poverty strategy will not succeed unless the local authority is able to co-operate with the local statutory bodies – particularly its district health authorities, and fire and passenger transport authorities. In the attack on poverty, health and safety, public protection and good communications are, after all, of fundamental importance.

(6) Finally, an anti-poverty strategy may falter because of the lack of an effective political will. The importance of council support is crucial. Without it policies may be approved but will then be put to one side and neglected. On the other hand, political commitment must be complemented fully by professional, officer support.

In spite of these difficulties, anti-poverty strategies are undoubtedly gathering strength around the country, demonstrating that many local authorities are determined to do more to assist the poorest members of their communities with improving their standards of living.

IV Key Issues in Anti-Poverty Strategy

In the review of the anti-poverty strategies of individual authorities in the previous chapter a number of practices emerged of common concern to local authorities, such as keeping fees and charges at reasonable levels, targeting, decentralising services, developing credit unions, improving debt recovery procedures, developing advice and advocacy and increasing the take-up of benefits. In the AMA survey some of these were reviewed under the general headings of income maintenance and support, decentralisation, economic development and welfare rights, with the forty-two participants responding with a wide range of information. Since the conclusion of the survey early in 1988 these issues have been researched more fully by the AMA's anti-poverty strategy working group, formed as a result of an increasing awareness of poverty issues amongst officers and councillors and stimulated in part by the research itself. This chapter attempts to summarise the accumulated knowledge collected through the survey and the case studies presented to the working group.

1. Income maintenance and support

1. Departmental responses

Although not normally involved with money as such, local authorities have methods at their disposal for assisting people on low incomes and thereby maintaining or raising income levels and enhancing basic living standards. Respondents to the AMA survey were asked therefore to list any measures being taken to enable people to obtain material or social goods and services at no charge or a reduced charge. Whilst responses came from a very wide range of departments with an equally diverse spread of schemes, the many departments giving a 'nil' response could be taken to indicate for some a low level of awareness, and for others, inactivity, on the poverty front.

The main responses to this part of the questionnaire were from social services, education, housing, recreation, libraries, environmental health and economic development departments. Below are the typical responses made:

Social services departments

Services for elderly people and people with disabilities included *no or low charges* for aids and minor adaptations, telephones, televisions, holidays, day centres and transport to and from these and home helps, emergency heating, luncheon clubs and meals on wheels. For children and families no or low charges were made for nurseries and family day centres and for a transfer to and from these. Section One payments were made to families with children; travelling expenses were paid for parents visiting children in care; support was given to clothing stores. In addition leaving care grants were made available to young people; grants were made to voluntary organisations helping poor people; free community transport and seed corn grants for community work were made available; parking and travel concessions were granted.

Education

In education there were free school meals for families in receipt of supplementary benefit and for other low income families (reduced since the 1986 Social Security Act to families receiving income support); nil charge for nurseries; rising five provision; reduced rentals for play groups; free use of schools accommodation for certain groups; reduction in cost of adult education; remission of library fines; free transport over certain distances and discretionary clothing grants for school uniform.

Housing

In housing there were many mechanisms for income maintenance and support including low rents policies; assistance with housing benefit; keeping rent arrears down and counselling those in arrears early on; insulation of dwellings to combat fuel poverty; support for MSC gardening/redecoration schemes; enhanced house renovation costs; decoration allowance; rental of garages below normal rates; sheltered units with free and heated communal areas and warden support not charged; free community halls on estates.

Leisure/Libraries

Departments concerned with leisure and libraries offered reduced charges for special groups including pensioners, unemployed people and handicapped people; 'passports' to leisure; concessionary fees for adult education; free hire of recreation halls; mini-bus service; free play facilities; all sorts of free clubs and holiday play schemes; free loan of art equipment, camping gear and kit; all library services free and mobile libraries and outreach services.

Environmental health

Measures in environmental health included the reduction of charges for extermination of wasps nests and rats, disinfestation and fumigation; hardship allowances for improvement grants and smoke control schemes.

Economic development

Economic development departments operated various schemes including travel concessions; a London taxi card scheme; cheap 'travel cards'; 'ring and ride' transport schemes; making recycled domestic goods available at a low cost. It was interesting to note that many of these activities which used to come under traditional local authority departments now come under the economic development heading.

Although these departments demonstrated a wide range of measures being taken to improve the lives of poor people, the responses indicated little co-ordination of thinking between departments in one authority, nor even consistency within a department. Only a few authorities, recognising this problem early on, had endeavoured to review their policies comprehensively – Camden being a case in point.

Since the poverty survey, the AMA has looked more closely into charging policies within social services departments, aware that changes in social security, the introduction of the social fund and changes suggested in the Griffiths report on Community Care are already leading to a questioning of the fees and charges being levied.

II. Fees and charges in social services departments

An AMA study, completed in June 1988, supplemented a similar study carried out in 1983 as well as the poverty survey. It showed no particular pattern of charging policies by region, size or type of authority amongst the

54 authorities who participated. Generally, however, whilst very few waived charges for all services, most did not charge for significant services such as aids and adaptations and home helps. All the evidence suggested that metropolitan authorities were attempting to keep charges down and that the range of charges had not kept pace with inflation. There was also an indication that more authorities were making nil assessments in 1988 than in 1983 and had resisted pressures to increase income. The low level of charges for meals or for cleaning services was clearly set at a level to reflect the low income levels of many of the recipients of these services. In that sense authorities had recognised that charging policies were an important part of anti-poverty strategies.

Nonetheless local authorities do not seem to have any coherent strategy whereby all their personal social services charges are considered for their impact on clients. One authority may for example consider it reasonable to charge for travel to and from a day centre, the cost of the meal, and a nominal attendance fee, but that same authority may not charge on a majority of other services. Aids to daily living seem to form a free service, or are at least on loan, whereas holidays for people with disabilities and elderly people seem almost universally to be charged for. Some authorities are even considering abandoning special holiday arrangements altogether. Most authorities seem to regard the charges which they levy for meals whether at home or in day centres to be reasonable (as indeed they are). Installation of telephones is still generally speaking free, in the spirit of the Chronically Sick and Disabled Persons Act 1970 and the charging policies for rentals and calls and the structure of charges have changed little in the period.

It is difficult to identify any more coherent pattern in charging policies from the material covered. Probably there is no coherence and maybe this is as it should be. It does allow local authorities the discretion to determine where they feel they can make most impact on poverty in their communities and assist low income families. However this study suggests that it would be useful for authorities to consider both in their social services and finance departments whether they should attempt to develop a more coherent strategy.

A few authorities have, in fact, already initiated action on this front. In Newcastle, for example, a charges working party met between August and November 1988 to examine social services charges in relation to the social services budget, to identify principles for a coherent and consistent charges policy and to identify issues which should be addressed corporately with particular reference to the developing anti-poverty strategy. The working party recognised that whilst charges could be used to raise revenue, some charges were not cost effective as they cost more to raise than they would accumulate. Collection costs could increase because of debt recovery. Therefore a balance had to be struck between the statutory requirement to levy a charge, the level of income which could be obtained and the cost of assessment and collection.

The effects of raising fees and charges have been illustrated elsewhere by studies of home help services. When charges are increased it is frequently the needy who drop out of the services or, if the service is retained, find it necessary to economise on food or heating. The preventative element of home care is thus diminished and may, in the long run, lead to greatly increased costs elsewhere, eg. in residential accommodation. Moreover charges may only amount to as little as 5% of the cost of the service apart from the cost of their collection outweighing their value.

Different departments do of course have very different procedures whereby they can assist income maintenance. The use of Section One of the Child Care Act 1980, further discussed in Chapter Five, is particular to social services, as are home improvement grants to housing or educational maintenance grants to education. Apart from social services, these will be considered in future AMA reports. What matters at the moment is to recognise that these could usefully fall within a coherent, corporate strategy systematically committed to relieving poverty.

How fees and charges are determined has to be closely connected to any 'targeting' policy. As fully discussed in the social services context in Chapter Five, targeting needs to be based in turn on knowledge of deprivation and those most affected. Without this selected 'targets' are unlikely to be reached. Frequently, as pointed out in Chapter Two, authorities do not have this knowledge – indeed they may even prefer not to have it as it might, as with the Disabled Persons Act 1986, for example, oblige them to meet needs for which they have inadequate resources.

2. Decentralisation

One approach developed for improving the take-up of services goes under the general label of 'decentralisation'. This is, however, a far more complex idea than the simple setting up of a neighbourhood office, or a patch-based social services team or a housing repairs unit, might suggest. It is closely related to that aspect of poverty conceptualised as powerlessness and is intended to give people greater access to and control over local services.

Decentralisation may be said to have emerged initially as a political and managerial solution for local government difficulties arising from the public's loss of confidence in local government services, recruitment and performance problems among some local authority staff, particularly in inner London boroughs, and lack of adequate transport to and from existing facilities. The ideology behind it goes beyond these practical issues, however, to a concern with 'consumerism' and the 'empowerment' of the consumer, two concepts in which an individual's choice of service and control over his/her living standards are seen as crucial. Issues of importance in this context for local authorities include service access; service delivery mechanism and the interface between customer and provider; service co-ordination at the local level; service delivery performance and participation and power (*Evans F, 1989*).

Most authorities participating in the AMA survey would appear to have taken up some of these issues in a few departments – notably social services and housing, but hardly any had developed decentralisation in a serious way. Islington has been one of the pioneers. Its twenty-four neighbourhood offices each with a population of about 6,500 contain the major services of housing, social services, environmental health and building works. Whilst each officer has no overall manager in order to encourage co-ordination between departments, a decentralisation co-ordinating unit, based in the chief executive's department provides a research and information source as well as a pool of specialists in personnel, financial and welfare rights matters. Each neighbourhood office is also the site of a local forum giving voice to local people and enabling them to become involved in local decision-making; a number of places in each forum is reserved for groups often under-represented in council affairs.

The decentralisation process is, however, fraught with difficulties. Decentralisation is expensive. It requires the refurbishment of old buildings and the provision of new ones, establishing an appropriate computer system and recruiting extra staff. Whilst there is evidence that policies such as Islington's will improve service take-up, this may be as much due to improved staff training and teamworking as to decentralisation per se and there is no clear proof that neighbourhood offices will result in a devolution of power to local people (*Willmott, 1989*). Neighbourhood office structures may in fact exclude tenants' associations, black organisations and consumers' groups, and dilute their power. The voluntary sector may also be marginalised (*Hoggett and Hambleton, 1987*). Further difficulties in the decentralisation process may also arise through internal resistance from senior officers, trade unions and other vested interests in local authorities as noted in Manchester between 1982 and 1984 (*Stoker, 1988*).

In evaluating the importance of a full programme of decentralisation for a local authority, Evans has argued that without moving towards a full neighbourhood office structure, it should still be possible to develop some of the policies and ideas created under the decentralisation umbrella which seem most to improve service efficiency and effectiveness. These may include: better reception facilities, closer links between housing and social services, more generic working for all grades of staff which could give rise to enhanced advice information services based on existing area offices, and increased local financial management of non-staffing costs. Many authorities could put such ideas to good use without a full programme of decentralisation. In Newcastle, for example, the Civic Centre is a centrally located, modern building; some key services are decentralised already and the city's priority area team system represents an established approach to involving local people in local authority matters. What is said to be lacking, however, is generic working between departments at the service delivery end. To fill this gap, the creation of a 'one stop shop service' for a range of enquiries and services at existing council offices is being considered as a possible answer, though even this limited move could be expensive.

There is still inadequate information available on the value of decentralisation. Some critics are openly sceptical (*eg. Beresford & Croft, 1986*). Even where access to services does improve, local control and the extension of local democracy seem fairly unlikely to result. More research is needed on this controversial but nevertheless popular idea and on its role within anti-poverty strategy.

3. Economic development

I. Economic development strategies

Local authorities have been involved in economic development since the last century when, for example, the first municipal gas works and council building programmes were initiated. Since the late 1970s, however, with the onset of the recession, high rates of unemployment and central government cuts in spending on regional policy, local authorities have become much more involved in efforts to boost their local economies. Their concern has focused particularly on the need to maintain and increase the rate base of their area by attracting new business and more jobs. Thus their activities have tended to be 'business' or 'property' led rather than focused on regenerating deprived areas or helping people especially vulnerable to unemployment, low pay and poor conditions of work. Whilst it should be perfectly possible to combine an approach which focuses on attracting new business and industry into an area, with one which emphasises helping vulnerable groups, in practice an emphasis on the former often takes place at the expense of the latter, as the experience of American urban development and, more recently, of London's Docklands have graphically illustrated. Major projects often attract skilled labour and specialists, sometimes from far afield, into deprived areas, rather than provide employment for the indigenous poor (*Southwark, 1989*).

The main source of financing for such activities has been the 1972 Local Government Act which made provision under Section 137 for a twopenny rate for miscellaneous local authority services. This has provided resources for both economic development and welfare rights activities. The value of this has been eroded by inflation, with most authorities reaching the limit of their spending powers. They have found additional resources in a variety of ways, in particular through partnership with central government in urban programme schemes for priority areas, through development programmes, 'Safer Cities' campaigns and task forces and through the European Social Fund. Financing has thus become increasingly difficult and complex.

Major changes are imminent, however, both under the Local Government and Housing Act which comes into force in April 1990 and with the reform of the community charge for business. Firstly, the Local Government and Housing Act has a specific economic development power and requires that local authorities wishing to undertake economic development publish a strategy and consult main business interests in their area. Secondly, the reform of the business rate will cease to contribute directly to local authority finance, but it will be paid to central government and then reallocated within a new revenue support system according to central government's estimates of local authorities' needs. This may result in less local authority concern simply to keep and attract any sort of business. These two developments, taken together, could encourage local authorities to take a broader view of economic development and target their activities more precisely on deprived areas and vulnerable groups of people.

Currently in local authorities economic development may take place in several different types of departments, including estates departments, planning departments, chief executive's departments and finance departments as well as economic development units. Responses to the AMA survey confirmed this distribution, but also showed some relevant activities in housing, education and social services. Few authorities appeared to have an economic strategy. Most were concerned on a piecemeal basis with assisting unemployed people by advising them on the options open to them, helping them move into self-employment or promoting innovative types of business ventures such as co-operatives and developing or supporting training schemes, many for people from ethnic minorities or people with disabilities. Local authorities had also worked closely with MSC training schemes, later replaced by the Employment Training Programme (ET), and with the Youth Training Scheme (YTS). There is now real concern that ET places are to be cut by 150,000 in 1990 and cuts are to be made in both the ET and YTS budgets (Chancellor's autumn statement 15.11.89). Central government has justified these cuts by the 25% fall in unemployment and 30% fall in long term unemployment in 1989 as well as by the fall in the numbers of young people joining the job market because of the downward demographic trend. Local authorities are only too aware, however, that national average trends are not necessarily reflected in the most deprived areas of boroughs. There is also concern that the eventual replacement of the Training Agency with Training and Enterprise Councils around the country, which will deliver TA services at the local level, will considerably restrict what local authorities can do in the field of training, promoting enterprise and, possibly, in economic development and urban regeneration.

Another aspect of economic development with which local authorities have been concerned has been 'planning gain'. Under this, part of the increased value of land released for development is passed on by developers to its local council for community use. Most planning gain is achieved, however, in reasonably attractive, central areas and not in the deprived areas where funds are most badly needed. In these areas developers and new businesses are likely to be put off by obvious evidence of vandalism, litter and graffiti and general dereliction. Local authorities, working with organisations such as Business in the Community, have been seeking ways, therefore, of attracting development and funds to areas previously deemed undesirable. This has provoked the realisation that such regeneration needs inputs from social services, housing and education and leisure departments as well as from economic development units in order to have any hope of success. In other words a corporate, anti-poverty strategy is needed.

Manchester is an example of an authority in which a co-ordinated development strategy, closely linked to the corporate anti-poverty strategy, has been promoted. The economic development programme revolves around several small project based teams. There is a special focus on training for employment, on developing the city centre itself into which 100,000 people come daily to work and on setting up a team in the chief executive's department to tackle privatisation and job losses. In the past 'the poor' have been seen as a homogeneous group, but now in Manchester appreciation of different categories of poverty has led to three urgent kinds of action, including the improving of services, changing the way the council operates and the creation of a development plan. Services are being improved through, for example, campaigns to change the attitudes of employers to young people and to establish good wage rates for those coming off YTS or its equivalent; schemes for ethnic communities are being launched as in Moss Side. Area offices have been targeted for surgeries in advice on training and on setting up businesses. Changes in the way the council operates are under consideration, including policy guidance to all chief officers that they should try to demonstrate an awareness of the effect of their policies on unemployed and wageless people, and a scheme to develop joint structures whereby policies for unemployed and wageless people and anti-poverty strategies are jointly reviewed. Beyond this a coherent agenda is being prepared to provide a development plan, of 2 to 5 years duration, to respond to the needs of the poor, and particularly the needs of unemployed and low waged people. In this context the development of local action teams of about 8 to 12 workers have been significant.

Economic development in Manchester has been faced not just with the demise of manufacturing but also with the loss of jobs in the service sector and slow rates of replacement. Eight new banks, opened between 1986 and 1989, have only needed to employ 42 people. In all 2,000 jobs have gone in banking and finance. As the main areas of employment growth in Manchester are in food, leisure, retailing and the media, it is likely that employment patterns will continue to change, making it important to monitor the effects of part-time work, shift work, and job sharing in these contexts, particularly on low pay. Manchester has instituted regular meetings with major employers, such as the big stores in growth areas and, in return for development finance, is arguing, with union support, for good pay levels. Manchester's experience indicates that, contrary to popular opinion in economic development, local authorities can have effective bargaining power. Manchester has also looked critically at its own role as a local employer and is endeavouring to open up career possibilities for its lowest paid employees.

II. Credit unions

In an analysis of local economic development in the mid-1980s, John Sellgren noted that there had been a growth of community based schemes whereby local people had joined together to develop community enterprises (*Sellgren, 1987*). Birmingham, for example, instituted a community development feasibility fund, a co-operative development agency, and a credit union development agency. Credit unions have attracted increasing interest over the last few years and many authorities are now beginning to view them as a sound way of increasing both saving and spending within the local economy as well as going some way to helping people in debt. In Birmingham in 1986 there were three credit unions, two employee based and one based on a common bond, with 1500 members and total assets of £3,000. By 1989, with the support of Birmingham's credit union development agency, members had increased in number to 4000 and assets had multiplied to over £1 million with a turnover in excess of £2 million.

A cautionary note, however, has been sounded by Richard Berthoud in a recent analysis of credit union development in the United Kingdom. Firstly, he has argued, whilst it is true that credit unions can provide cheap loans, with their rates of 1% per month or 12.7% per annum, about half that of banks and building societies, it has to be remembered that credit union members have to borrow their own money and cannot draw out their savings. Taking that into account, credit unions lending rates are only marginally the cheapest. Secondly, whilst credit unions appear to save their members from the clutches of money lenders, it is hard to substantiate this. It is also surprising to discover that members have more savings in banks and other institutions than they have in credit unions and individuals circulate more money through mainstream credit. Thirdly, although credit unions are seen as institutions for poor people, some contain very few who could be called poor. Savings are largely contributed by the better off who also borrow the larger amounts. Thus credit union funds have a tendency, in spite of intentions, to gravitate towards the better off. Against this it is clear that credit unions offer people the opportunity to save in small quantities, the opportunity to borrow in small quantities over a short period, and the chance to develop in personal confidence whilst working for the community.

Local authorities face a number of problems in attempting to support the development of credit unions. The 1979 Credit Union Act imposed legal restraints on levels of membership, saving and lending, and these can prove restrictive, as can the limited interpretation that is required of the 'common bond' – the requirement that those forming a credit unit all know one another and live in a well defined geographical area. Funding is a further difficulty, although central government can help with this through, for example, urban aid programmes. At the moment there seems to be no national policy on this. Credit union development also requires years of support, and authorities cannot expect to put a worker in situ for say 12 months and achieve good results.

Credit unions are unique in that they should undoubtedly fit into a local authority's anti-poverty strategy on both economic and social grounds. Their value in mitigating debt and encouraging local saving and spending is seen to be of an importance equal only to their capacity to empower individuals and challenge the lack of control from which poor people so often suffer. It is not clear however where exactly credit union development should feature within a corporate strategy. In Manchester and Waltham Forest, for example it is established within economic development, undoubtedly an appropriate location, but EDUs do not always figure significantly in anti-poverty strategies and may not see the need to encourage communication between for example, money advice agencies and credit union development agencies. If credit union development is to work effectively in an authority, therefore, it needs to have inter-departmental recognition and support so that those who most need the help that a credit union can offer are made aware of the advantages and assisted with taking them up. It also needs to be seen as part of a wider spectrum of effort aimed at improving and maintaining the circulation of money in the local economy. In this latter context benefit take-up campaigns have proved valuable with a capacity to bring thousands of extra pounds into deprived areas. (*Finister, 1986.*)

The many problems which economic development addresses are indicative of the importance of inter-departmental work in economic development in general. At the moment there is little evidence of economic development units working collaboratively with any other departments and this is something which the future development of anti-poverty strategies should seek to redress. Given the differing ideology involved, however, in creating new business and in meeting the employment needs of, for example, people with disabilities and those who are mentally ill, this will be no easy task.

4. Welfare rights

Since Manchester appointed the first welfare rights officer in 1972 and subsequently established the first welfare rights team, local authority support for benefit and money advice services has been greatly extended. By the mid 1980s at least 65 councils in Great Britain directly employed welfare rights specialists, including 37 metropolitan authorities, with the service noticeably concentrated in London's inner city boroughs and in the major conurbations (*Berthoud, 1986*). In addition, most local authorities were providing grant aid to independent advice agencies, including housing advice services, consumer advice centres, neighbourhood advice centres, family advice centres and law centres. In fact some authorities, like North Tyneside, had deliberately appointed just one council-based welfare rights worker to stimulate their local network of agencies, although others, like Manchester and Newcastle, had developed in-house services to act as the co-ordinating hub of a system of decentralised advice services (*Fimister, 1986*).

Local authority welfare rights work is concerned not just with the take-up of benefits, but also with general advice and advocacy, community development, publicity, training and policy orientated work. Whatever its focus, however, it is overwhelmingly involved with people on low incomes and has proved in many cases to be the source from which the drive to develop a corporate anti-poverty strategy has originated. With their main concerns for income maintenance and citizens' financial rights, welfare rights services would seem to be an obvious base from which an anti-poverty strategy could be developed.

Recent events have demonstrated, however, that the limited size and resources of welfare rights teams, as well as the growing demand on their basic services, have made it difficult for them to devote sufficient time to anti-poverty strategy to render it viable on a corporate level. Twenty-one of thirty-seven welfare rights units known to exist in the metropolitan authorities responded to the AMA survey. Most operated small teams of between four and eight officers although there were a few exceptions such as Bradford, Islington and Manchester with over 20 officers. As Berthoud noted, budgets were unpredictable, with some financed from departmental budgets throughout the authority and others with their own budgets totalling anything between £43,000 and £550,000.

Small teams with limited budgets have been particularly badly placed to do anything more than cope with the marked increase in individual benefit and debt inquiries that have taken place in the 1980s. The AMA survey into the impact of unemployment on the personal social services (Balloch et al, 1985) had found a marked increase in welfare rights referrals in the early 1980s which was directly attributed to unemployment. Since then changes in benefit resulting from the implementation of the 1986 Social Security Act and the replacement of DSS single payments by the social fund have resulted in many more benefit enquiries whilst increasing indebtedness has particularly required the development of specialist debt services. Unsurprisingly, all evidence shows that many debtors are social security claimants (*Berthoud, 1989*) whose debts are more commonly for gas and electricity bills and housing costs. In a recent snapshot study of the existing social work clients and new referrals of 26 authorities carried out in a target week in October 1988, Becker revealed a multitude of different types of financial problems. Over one third of current clients experienced general DSS problems and nearly one in five needed a benefit assessment; most new referrals had DSS problems with a need for benefit assessment and help with rent and furniture. These social work clients came from the most vulnerable groups in society, people with disabilities, mentally ill and elderly people, and many more under 25 (*Becker, Feb 1989*).

Local studies have shown that loss of benefits following the 1986 Act has been a major contributor to this situation. Cleveland County Council's report *For Richer For Poorer* estimated that over 9,000 claimants of income support had suffered a reduction in real terms in their benefits since April 1988. Middlesbrough Council reported that 600 council tenants lost entitlement to housing benefit and a further 9,300 lost benefit of between £2 and £15 per week. In 1986 £7.6 million was paid out by 5 local DSS offices in single payment grants but the social fund budget for 1988/9 was only £1.03 for the 5 offices. Thus it seems that a total of over £20 million in benefits may have been lost each year to a county in which unemployment remains consistently high.

Given such situations around the country – and whilst Cleveland may be in the worst of categories, it is not unique – it is understandable that welfare rights officers are shouldering an increasingly heavy workload. In this context, to take on the development of an anti-poverty strategy could normally only result in the strategy not being properly implemented or sustained at the expense of some other priority. On the other hand it is clear that the role of welfare rights is crucial in the development of any anti-poverty strategy. Firstly, welfare rights officers are in a unique position to gain and disseminate knowledge of their local communities and the income and housing difficulties experienced by individuals. The AMA survey did show, however, that most welfare rights units do not keep easily accessible records of the latter and this might be something for future consideration. Secondly, welfare rights officers have an important role to play in the training and education of local officers. This point has been forcibly made in a recent CCETSW paper in which the importance of a welfare rights education for social workers was emphasised. This would clarify the extent to which the problems of many individuals are basically those of impoverishment and would serve as a balance to the case work approach with its focus on relationships and individual inadequacies (*Stewart J. ed., 1989*). Thirdly, welfare rights officers as a group have been distinguished by their energy and awareness of policy and strategic issues within their authorities. They are more prepared and more able than most to give expression to the key concerns of anti-poverty strategy – the redirection of scarce resources to those in greatest need.

In spite of all this, one must reiterate that the size and scope of most welfare rights units makes it impossible for them to provide the administrative resources which an anti-poverty strategy requires. Moreover, welfare rights units are themselves often marginalised by their position within an authority's bureaucracy – within social services departments for example – and this could lead to the marginalisation of the strategy as a whole. It may be preferable, therefore, for an anti-poverty strategy to be based in either the chief executive's department or in a development department with the strongest possible input of knowledge and advice from welfare rights. (*See Chapter Six.*)

5. Conclusion

This chapter has briefly reviewed some of the key issues which have emerged over the last few years as important to the development of an anti-poverty strategy. The case studies presented in Chapter Three had already illustrated these to some extent, but it was necessary to examine them in greater detail in order to expose both the difficulties and pressures to which they are suspect. In the future it will partly be the development of effective policies – within the fields of income maintenance, decentralisation, economic development and welfare rights – which will determine the relative success or failure of anti-poverty strategy in local government. Much will also, however, depend on relationships between central and local government, as discussed in the sixth and final chapter.

welfare of children by diminishing the need to receive children into care or to bring them before a juvenile court; and any provision made by a local authority under the subsection may, if the local authority thinks fit, include provision for giving assistance in kind, or in exceptional circumstances, in cash.'

The AMA survey showed that, prior to 1988, some social services departments were already increasing their use of Section One payments in response to the cutting of DSS single payments. Following the survey, the local authority associations (AMA and ACC) sent a questionnaire to their members in April 1988 to seek further statistical material about budgets for Section One payments for 1987/88 and 1988/89. Sixty-five authorities responded to the questionnaire (forty-two metropolitan authorities and twenty-three county councils) giving a 66% response rate for all English and Welsh social services authorities. The metropolitan authorities reported an 8.5% increase in

Table I
AMA/ACC Section 1 Survey* 1988

Areas	1987/88			1988/89		
	Section One Payments	Total Child Care Budget	Section One Payments as % of Total Child Care Budget	Section One Payment	Total Child Care Budget	Section One Payments as % of Total Child Care Budget
	£	£		£	£	
Metropolitan Districts (42)*	2m	154.70m	1.3%	2.17m	162.9m	1.3%
% Annual Increase				8.5%	5.3%	
County Councils (23)*	1.84m	122.80m	1.5%	2.08m	134.57m	1.5%
% Annual Increase				13%	9.5%	
TOTAL	3.84m	277.50m	1.4%	4.25m	297.47m	1.4%
% Annual Increase				10%	7.2%	

* Figures only for complete run of figures on all headings when given by local authorities

expenditure for 1988/89, the county councils 13%. There were, however, wide variations between authorities, as previous surveys had also indicated (*Stewart & Stewart, 1989*). Metropolitan authorities recorded estimated payments ranging from £3,000 in one authority to £525,700 in another in 1988/89. In the counties in this same year figures ranged from £13,000 to £325,000. Although the amounts involved in Section One payments are comparatively small when seen against the total child care budget of £500 million, and more so against the £3 billion personal social service budget, these payments are crucial to the destitute families who receive them.

In answering the questionnaire, the majority of authorities said that they had reviewed or were about to review their policy on Section One payments. Their responses reflected their increasing concern both for firmer budgetary control and for meeting the needs of families for whom DSS single payments were no longer available, social fund loans unmanageable, and social fund grants refused. Review of Section One payments policies have included an emphasis on establishing good lines of communication with voluntary organisations, advocating on the client's behalf and continuing to make clear to social security officers where the limit of local authority responsibility lies. In that regard most authorities appear to have adopted *Social Fund – Practice Guide and Position Statement (AMA/ACC, 1988)*.

In the future it seems likely that, for poor families, the balance between income support and Section One payments may be crucial, with social workers unwillingly, but increasingly, involved in the business of income maintenance. Section 17 of the Children Act 1989, which places a general duty on every local authority to safeguard and promote the welfare of children in need in their area and to promote the upbringing of such children by their families, by providing a range and level of services, including assistance in kind or in cash, poses the issue even more clearly[1].

II. Children in care

Although a review of Section One payment policy may indicate a social services department's awareness of the importance of its own response to poverty, the AMA survey revealed paradoxes and contradictions in departmental policies and attitudes. Take for example evidence from the AMA survey of support from social services departments for the parents of children in care and parental contributions. The majority of children coming into care are from social classes 4 and 5 with a disproportionate number from an ethnic minority background (*Short Report, 1984*). Most are therefore from poor families with parents who can ill afford the travelling and telephone costs that may be involved in keeping in contact with their children. Almost all respondents said that they provided financial assistance for travel costs to the families of children in care by a variety of methods; some said they had a

1 A fuller discussion of Section One payments may be found in 'Benefits Research', the Bulletin of the Social Fund Project, Nottingham Benefits Research Unit, Issue Three, B Jones, July 1989.

special 'children in care' fund or budget, others specifically referred to the use of Section One money. Only two authorities said they made no formal provision at all. *charging for children in care*

In spite of this recognition of need the same authorities demonstrated a surprising determination to secure parental contributions towards the costs of keeping children in care. Under the Health and Social Services and Social Security Adjudications Act, 1983, local authorities are empowered to charge parents for keeping their children in care up to the amount of the weekly boarding out rate. However, an authority need not serve a contribution notice 'in any case where in the circumstances they consider it unreasonable to require contributions.' (*HSSSSA, Clause 19(3)*). Among respondents only three said they did not charge parents at all. The others did not charge parents receiving supplementary benefit but charged the rest according to a variety of means tests and sliding scales. Whereas some would charge no more than the weekly child benefit of £7.25, others went by the letter of the law and charged an amount equivalent to that paid to foster parents, for example £28.70 to £57.33 per week according to the child's age. It was possible for some parents to be charged up to one third of their income.

Where parents defaulted on payments, most authorities cited court action as a likely step and had a standard set of procedures which built up to this. Whereas court action to recover Section One loans is never taken, court action to enforce parental contributions seemed to be much more commonplace. Yet the parents of children in care are known to be generally poor and recognised as such. There is here an inconsistency in both policy and practice towards poor people encouraged by relevant pieces of legislation that at the time of the AMA survey only a handful of authorities had recognised (*Balloch and Jones, 1988*). Such inconsistency was also evident in policies on fees and charges discussed in Chapter Four. *leaving care (CA)*

An earlier AMA study (*Balloch et al, 1985*) provided evidence of the hardship being experienced by children leaving care, many in areas of widespread unemployment. Since then the situation has deteriorated because income support levels are clearly insufficient to support a young person living alone. There is growing evidence across the country of a cycle of poverty, homelessness, unemployment, drug and alcohol misuse and prostitution among the 8,000 18 year olds leaving care each year and the unknown number of 16 and 17 year olds. A recent study (*Newman, 1989*) found that, of 532 young people who had left home and linked up with the Central London Teenage Project, 34% came from local authority care. As less than 1% of young people in the United Kingdom, aged 0–18 years, were in care in 1989, this was a worrying percentage. Under the Children Act, 1989, the continuing power for local authorities to advise, assist and befriend children leaving their care has been reinforced (Section 24). The local authority associations are still considering the resource implications of this. For social services departments this will comprise a significant element in anti-poverty strategy.

2. Targeting

Over twenty years ago, the Seebohm report recommended that social services departments concern themselves with both the prevention of hardship and the targeting of priority areas. (*Seebohm Report 1968, Chapters XIV, XVI.*) Evidence from the AMA survey suggests that to some extent social services departments are doing this with great difficulty given their lack of resources and shortage of staff.

Targeting requires both statistical and local knowledge of where needs are most pressing. Few authorities approach the task of acquiring this in an organised way, through, for example, poverty profiles, but rely on 'commonsense' and their general knowledge of deprived estates and areas. This may not only result in overlooking deprived localities, such as those characterised by low quality, privately rented accommodation, but can also result in the neglect of deprived individuals scattered in more affluent areas and communities isolated by language difficulties. Moreover, area targeting seldom works unless carried out in conjunction with other departments, especially housing and education and this is not always attempted.

As with central government efforts to target deprivation, local authority area targeting may also be characterised by a paternalism that can ultimately only reinforce dependency on benefits and services rather than empower people to take control of their own lives. This is where 'community development', rather than a concentration on 'priority areas' may prove a more useful approach (*AMA, Community Development: The Local Authority Role, 1989*).

The AMA survey, which looked at departmental responses to specifically vulnerable groups, showed how not only social services departments, but also housing and education departments, try to target particular types of clients. Responses indicated that clear choices were made by departments of the sorts of clients who should receive 'priority treatment' and of those who were the prime responsibility of social services, or of others. Departments were asked about the 'priority treatment' being given by them to any of fifteen categories of people. These groups, whilst not ideal, were identified according to CIPFA categories in the first instance and their significance in local authority work confirmed in the pilot surveys in Southwark and Richmond. They included the under fives; children in care; single parent families; the elderly; physically or sensorily handicapped adults; mentally handicapped adults; the homeless; women; ethnic minorities; the low paid; the unemployed; the chronically ill; drugs and alcohol users and carers. 'Priority treatment' was defined as 'the special allocation of funds, staff resources, premises and/or services made to ease the material and social deprivation of the groups in question'. Such treatment would take departments beyond the bounds of statutory obligation and could reasonably be construed as targeting.

A handful of authorities said that in all fairness they could not respond to the AMA's questions because they were concerned in one way or another with all the groups mentioned. One, for example, said that its growing emphasis on an enhanced role for domiciliary services meant offering a more intensive level of support across a wider range of client groups, with improved services for carers an integral component of this. The fact that only about four authorities made this type of comment does suggest, however, that targeting whether structured, ad hoc, or informal is a general practice which is understood in most departments. Just one of the departments which could not respond said that it did in fact have a specific policy of non-targeting so that 'growth' will spread evenly amongst its consumers with no one group benefiting at the expense of others.

The material analysed showed that where groups are seen as the special responsibility of a particular department, they may receive little special consideration from other departments. Some groups appeared to receive widespread attention across departments and other groups were apparently not targeted by anybody. In social service departments it was the under-fives and the elderly who were most likely to receive priority treatment with the least likely being homeless people, the low paid, women, the unemployed, the chronically ill and drugs and alcohol users. In itself this was interesting as the under-fives is a category where social services have only a limited statutory responsibility, whereas elderly people are covered by a wide range of statutory powers and duties. Both, however, are groups where demographic pressures are building up. Housing departments appeared to place homeless people at the top of their list and the under-fives at the bottom although social services departments perceived the needs of these groups and their responsibility in meeting those needs in exactly the opposite way. The quality of the material on which these observations were based is, however, open to several interpretations. It could, nevertheless, suggest that departments are highly likely to see some special groups of people as their particular responsibility and to leave the needs of other groups to other departments. The departmentalism that this targeting reflects runs the risk of encouraging a blinkered approach in which people's needs are not conceived as a related set of problems but are only partially emphasised. Do, for example, the housing needs of homeless people remain unrelated to the social and educational deprivation and the health problems from which homeless families are known to suffer?

Some groups, such as elderly people and those with disabilities (often overlapping), receive special treatment in both housing and social services departments. There is evidence that there may be some groups of people who are not thought to merit special treatment at all. These include women, the low paid and unemployed, the chronically ill, drugs and alcohol abusers. Is it that these are classified as the 'undeserving poor'? Ethnic minorities also receive a low level of priority treatment (mentioned by less than half the departments in either case), although evidence of their particular problems has been well documented (*e.g. Cheetham, 1982; Dominelli, 1989*).

As with area targeting, assessments of need are dependent on accurate information about the location, income levels and particular requirements of the groups in question. Without local surveys, such information is simply not available to support the decision-making process. Local authorities have, however, shown how successfully they can obtain such information – Camden's survey of disabled people (*op cit, Chapter Two*) and their carers and Tameside's study of elderly, ethnic minority people, being cases in point.

This discussion shows that both area and group targeting has its pitfalls. It requires not only accurate information but also an understanding approach to meeting need in which empowerment and an emphasis on rights outweighs paternalism. It also requires decisions on the levels of fees and charges so that those in need are not barred from essential services (*Chapter Four*).

3. The under fives

There appears to be widespread agreement on the main problems faced by certain groups, particularly the 'under-fives' and 'the elderly' – the two groups which are most likely to be receiving priority treatment. A rise in the number of under-fives in many areas was reported and this was said to be reflected in the growth of day nursery waiting lists, some of which had doubled between 1986 and 1988. An increased demand for child minders was also regularly mentioned. Along with this was a reported increase in the number of under-fives living in poverty with children said to be poorly dressed, poorly nourished and sometimes neglected. Some authorities said that their figures for children received into care were going down – reflecting a national trend – although the length of stay of some under-fives in care was causing concern, but others reported an increase in numbers received into care coupled with, or because of, an increase in the numbers of child abuse referrals. Problems were being made worse by a lack of resources for adequate remuneration for play group leaders and the inability of parents to afford nursery fees. This inability was directly related to unemployment and low levels of pay. Communities were said to be very willing and ready to organise their own nursery resources but were hampered by their lack of finance.

High on the list of local authority responses to this range of problems was the increase of nursery provision. In spite of the serious lack of resources, this was being achieved in a number of ways. Authorities were developing nursery satellites in high need localities with flexible services, building new nurseries and increasing the number of free places in day nurseries, whilst increasing the weekly fee to sponsored child minders. Grants to the Playgroup Association and to other major voluntary organisations such as Save the Children and a large number of small 'seedcorn' grants were given to various voluntary organisations to enable play groups to be established. Some authorities said they were changing the function of day care from that of day nurseries to family centres.

The significance of such initiatives has been supported by recent research at the National Institute for Social Work (NISW) where Jane Gibbons has been examining the impact of poverty on families with young children who are referred to social services. She interviewed 143 parents of children under 14 referred to area teams in two Southern counties and compared these with 359 randomly selected parents in the same age group from similar communities. There were striking differences between referred families and other families in the local community. 70% of referred families lacked a wage earner compared with only 12% of the community families. From a number of indicators – absence of wage earner, poor housing, lack of consumer goods and large family size it was found that under 10% of those referred had no disadvantage indicators whilst 32% of community families had none. Nearly half referred had three or more indicators of disadvantage compared to only 8% of community families. Of referred families 57% experienced considerable social disadvantage, and had many urgent financial problems. (*Gibbons, 1989.*)

Although social services departments can have little influence on national policies affecting employment, housing or benefits for mothers and children, they are directly in touch with a sizeable proportion of the most severely disadvantaged families with young children, and so are in a favourable position to use their limited resources to offer help.

Given that 46% of the most disadvantages have never had any pre-school experience compared to only 10% of the most advantages, (*Osborne A F and Millbank J E 'The Effects of Early Education' Oxford: Clarendon Press, 1987*), local authorities should use their powers to provide and support day care services for under fives. Indeed the provisions in the Children Act 1989 underlines those powers though at this stage Government appears unwilling to add the resources local government will argue it needs.

In fostering and adoption the AMA survey showed that some authorities were pursuing a 'permanency policy' to ensure that children were rehabilitated with their families within a six month period or placed for adoption. Additional staff were being provided for some children's homes. Child protection teams were being developed. Some authorities were also able to illustrate how the problems of departmentalism in provision for the under-fives were being surmounted. In Leeds, a nursery committee had been established to consider matters related to provision by social services, education and the voluntary sector. Other authorities also reported joint working parties with education. Such measures can be seen as examples of good preventative action by local government.

4. The elderly

It is to be expected that priority treatment will be accorded by social services departments to elderly people with over 80% of departments recording the elderly as a group receiving special treatment and over half of these perceiving the problems of the elderly as increasing in their severity. The problems of the elderly were universally defined as those of scarce resources for an increasingly dependent service user group. An illustration of this was given by Coventry. In Coventry referrals to the social services department of elderly people had risen from 4,236 in the 1981/82 period to 6,299 in the 1986/87 period. The rate of referral per 1,000 of the elderly population had risen 96.6 to 136.0. The proportion of the 85 plus was expected to rise by 52% in the next ten years. In Coventry also a survey of ethnic minority elderly people had shown that 67% were between 55 and 65 yers of age but only 8% over 75 years of age. Demand therefore was expected to increase dramatically in the 1990s. Over and above the increased demand being generated by demographic factors were the problems caused by inadequate heating, low income, and a lack of necessary transport. These problems had in turn provoked a high demand for day care which had resulted in local authorities having long waiting lists. The problems of those caring for elderly people had also increased and support for carers was regarded as a priority. Evidence from other parts of the survey also showed that support for carers was steadily growing.

In their increasing provision for the elderly, social services departments regularly mentioned their joint work with housing departments and health authorities, showing that in this example departmentalism was being surmounted. Perhaps Care in the Community policies were taking effect, albeit gradually, and in advance of action on Griffiths. Activities included the development of sheltered or very sheltered housing with increases in staffing, the development of resource centres into targeted areas, the upgrading of old people's homes to bring them up to 'Home Life' standards, the expansion of day services, the improvement and extension of domiciliary services, including a free home help service, plans to combat hypothermia, the distribution of information to extend the elderly's knowledge of available service, and the provision of grants to many voluntary organisations such as Pensioners Link.

These examples of information obtained from the AMA's survey give an indication of the enormous range of services that local authorities are attempting to provide to groups such as the under-fives and the elderly who are amongst those in particular danger from poverty. In contrast, there are other groups of people, whose needs many might argue are pressing, who are not receiving such support or attention. In the survey, for example, no social services department and no department of environmental health made any mention of special provisions being made to target those infected by HIV and those living with AIDS.

In the case of this group, only housing departments seemed to be making any progress in provision. Since the survey, however, considerable development is known to have taken place (*AMA, 1988, 1989*). The Local Authority Associations' Officer Working Group on AIDS has been engaged since 1988 in providing comprehensive guidance for local authorities on the implications of HIV for all departments and crucially have identified the disproportionate impact which recent changes in social security legislation have had on people with HIV infection or AIDS.

What may be needed in the long run in each authority is an assessment of the priority treatment given to groups throughout all departments and an assessment of the extent to which such targeting corresponds with what is known about the needs of the groups in question.

5. People with disabilities

Social services departments are confronted by the problems of poverty in no uncertain terms in their care for people with disabilities. The recent OPCS reports on disability – the products of the new national surveys on disablement, have shown that there are at least twice as many disabled adults in Britain (6.5 million) as was previously officially estimated and some 360,000 disabled children (*OPCS*). The financial circumstances of these people fall well below that of the rest of the population, with three quarters of disabled adults in private households (4.3 million) relying on state benefits as their main source of income and 4.5 million living in households where there are no earners. Where disabled people do have jobs, their earnings are substantially lower than those of non-disabled employees and even the earnings of the parents of disabled children are below average. In addition disabled people have to bear many of the extra costs of clothing, heating and so forth incurred directly because of their disability. (*See also Disability Alliance, 1987.*)

The AMA's survey into the impact of unemployment on demand for the personal social services carried out in 1984 showed how employment opportunities for disabled people had declined in all the authorities surveyed (*Balloch et al, 1985*). Day centres and adult training centres were experiencing overcrowding and understaffing and clients were frustrated by waiting lists and transport difficulties. Responses to the later poverty survey have indicated a continuation of these difficulties in spite of a wide range of efforts to overcome them. Problems occur at both ends of the age scale. Young adults with disabilities leaving college often have little to which to look forward and services are increasingly strained to assist elderly disabled persons. Although a majority of pensioners are not disabled, the OPCS surveys did show that a majority of those aged 85 and over do have locomotor, hearing and personal care difficulties. Given the general impoverishment of this group, this means increasing demand for care and support from social services departments in the 1990s.

There is much concern over the impact of the changes brought into force in April 1988 as a result of the 1986 Social Security Act. The Disability Alliance argues that there have been cuts in living standards for over 1 million people with disabilities and severe cuts in many of these cases. As nearly half of all pensioners on supplementary benefit were disabled, some 347,000 disabled pensioners must have lost out in the changeover to income support as well as some 145,000 new pensioner adults. Changes in housing benefit resulted in over 5 million people losing some help with their rents and rates with the transitional protection scheme only assisting some 178,000, so disabled people were badly affected again. Low take up of family credit and the freezing of child benefit have since combined to make a bad situation even worse. The Disability Alliance has commented 'The best that can be said for the new social security system is that it has been an appalling failure as far as people with disabilities have been concerned, representing the most savage attack on their living standards' (*Disability Alliance, 1989*). It is against this background that social services departments are now called on to implement the provisions of the 1986 Disabled Persons Act as well as meet the requirements for adequate community care.

6. Conclusion

At the start of this chapter it was noted that social services departments have not usually provided the launching pad for a local authority anti-poverty strategy. Some have not even necessarily supported its development. There are several possible explanations for this, which include the possibility that social services departments are so accustomed to the poverty of their clients that they are almost inured to it, that they do not see themselves as having the necessary power and resources to do anything much about a situation which largely results from external economic forces, or that their proper role is to deal in relationships, not deprivation. Current developments, and especially the operation of the social fund, are more than likely, however, to push social services departments into the frontline of anti-poverty activity, whether they like it or not.

Social and demographic changes – the so-called demographic time bomb – seem set to increase the numbers of vulnerable people. A rising birthrate, particularly in inner city areas, and an increasing percentage of frail elderly people will put more demands on social services departments, not less. Increasing rates of divorce will almost certainly put more lone parents, (mainly women) and their children into poverty. Inadequate levels of benefit and pensions and low rates of pay for women will continue to make support from social services all the more essential. Legislative changes, placing more emphasis on the role of social services in supporting such groups, will require both thought and action. These include a wide range of changes including specifically changes in disability law, the implementation of the White Paper on Community Care and the Children Act and more generally the changes in local government organisation and finance emanating from the contracting out of services and the community charge.

In spite of this, it would be unfortunate for concern for poverty to be 'marginalised' into social services departments. The whole purpose of an anti-poverty strategy is to encompass activities throughout a local authority's departments making certain that key issues, such as those discussed in the previous chapter, are addressed by everybody. It is practical, therefore, for the central organisation of an anti-poverty strategy to be situated outside the social services department – in, for example, chief executive's, or economic development – whilst the social services department becomes increasingly aware and supportive of its aims along the lines considered.

This chapter has endeavoured to look at the contribution that a social services department may make to support a corporate anti-poverty strategy. As the AMA research was initiated and supported by the AMA's Social Services Committee, this discussion is particularly appropriate in this context, but it should not suggest any dismissal of the key roles of housing or education or other departments. These will be dealt with fully in a future review.

VI Local Government and Anti-Poverty Strategy in the 1990s

1. Anti-poverty strategy and the causes of poverty

An anti-poverty strategy can be thought of as a corporate strategy whereby scarce resources are aimed more directly towards poor people, services are made more accessible to them and greater control over their own living standards is made possible for them. As such, an anti-poverty strategy can equally well be located in a local authority, a health authority, or for that matter any statutory authority, in a voluntary organisation, or theoretically, even in a private, commercial or industrial enterprise. Procedures whereby statutory, voluntary, commercial and industrial bodies may work together in the name of anti-poverty can also evolve, as some of the case studies outlined in this text have indicated.

In some ways the term 'anti-poverty' is an unfortunate one because it sounds both reactive and defensive rather than progressive, but this does not warrant abandoning a phrase which has now gained a wide currency. In many ways anti-poverty strategies are indeed defensive reactions against what is seen as unreasonable behaviour by central government, both in its exaggeration of social divisions through economic and social policies and in its threatened emasculation of local government. If anti-poverty strategies are to make headway in the 1990s, however, there is a clear need for them to set goals and objectives which may be regarded as progressive and positive.

In local government, in order to do this, those involved in the development of anti-poverty strategy have to be clear, firstly, about what they mean by 'poverty' and, secondly, about how they define the 'causes of poverty'. This is not to say, however, that one narrow conception of poverty must dominate a strategy. A broad, relative definition, encompassing, as outlined in Chapter One, the concepts of income maintenance, lack of material and social resources, and powerlessness, will do well and can be adapted by individual departments wishing to make sense of the delivery of the goods and services for which they have responsibility. Thus whilst housing, education and social services departments, for example, will need to develop their own distinctive approaches to poverty, their underlying conceptions of the problems involved will need to be co-ordinated so that joint action can be taken where necessary.

Defining the causes of poverty involves recognising certain 'theories of poverty' which are rarely discussed, let alone made explicit amongst policy makers. Yet any solutions to the problems of poverty logically depend on the way in which the causes of poverty are analysed and no anti-poverty strategy can appeal sensibly to people if it does not distinguish at the outset between what are believed to be the causes of poverty and what are the symptoms, or the effects, of continuous deprivation. If, for example, individuals are seen as the sole architects of their own destinies, poverty has to be viewed as the consequence of personal inadequacy and failure and policies will concentrate on supporting and re-educating such people and, in particular, encouraging them to become 'independent'. If, however, economic and social forces are seen to be the root causes, policies aimed at reducing unemployment, improving low pay levels and restructuring social security will be more highly favoured.

In the 1960s a number of writers developed a concept which became known as the 'culture of poverty' (*e.g. Oscar Lewis, 1961, 1966*), coming to the conclusion that poor people had a distinctive attitude to life and developed a culture which was both alien to the mainstream culture of the society in which they existed and lacked stable community and family networks. Such thinking was incorporated into the USA's educational programme 'Operation Headstart' and reflected in Keith Joseph's thinking on the 'cycle of deprivation'. Many 'community development' initiatives in this country also built on the idea, seeing in the creation of community networks a strategy for attacking poverty but as Peter Willmott has recently observed: 'Community development projects, community action programmes and the like can help some individual participants to develop their capacities and perhaps move out of poverty, but the belief that such small-scale schemes could have any fundamental impact on social and economic structures has long been exposed as mistaken' (*Willmott, 1989*).

A concept similar in several ways to the 'culture of poverty' has also recently gained substantially in popularity – namely 'the underclass' (*Murray, 1989*). Within the underclass a growing band of alienated people are described as devastating inner city areas. The moral decline of the underclass is said to be reflected in a rising tide of idleness, illegitimacy, crime and vandalism, drug and alcohol use, none of which is seen as the result of poverty but rather, as the cause. If this is to be believed, welfare benefits will only make a bad situation worse, encouraging both dependency and a continuation of bad behaviour. Yet just as amongst poor people in Nottingham in the 1970s, Coates and Silburn found no trace of the 'culture of poverty' (*Coates and Silburn, 1970*), so there is little evidence that unemployed people, homeless people, single parents and others wish to opt out of British society. If an underclass exists at all, its members have been forced out of society rather than chosen to leave (*Field, 1989*).

Such a debate is a distraction from those racial and sexual divisions in society which continue to result in discrimination against ethnic minorities and women in the key fields of employment, housing, education and social security. Other discriminatory practices against disabled people, mentally ill people and elderly people are also prevalent. As an independent cause of poverty, discrimination is often overlooked or subsumed within some vague theory of class with little justification. This may be one reason why an equal opportunities policy is frequently not seen as an integral part of an anti-poverty strategy – yet the two belong together and need to co-ordinate their aims. Extending this debate on the causes of poverty may help to make this possible.

2. Practical steps towards anti-poverty strategy

The opening discussion on defining the nature and causes of poverty may have seemed rather an abstract exercise, but it was a necessary preliminary to establishing a framework within which the tangible and practical elements of a strategy could be worked out. A coherent programme could concentrate, for example on ten, quite precise exercises; all of which are illustrated in earlier chapters. All ten suggestions are documented in various places in this text as the references indicate. Beyond these there is great scope for further developments that this discussion has not been able to encompass – in joint activities with health authorities, transport authorities and police authorities for a start. In spite of the heavy restrictions being imposed by central government, imaginative and determined activity coupled with efficiency and industry could yet turn an anti-poverty strategy into reality:

- Developing and keeping up to date a poverty profile (Chapter Two).
- Co-ordinating benefit services, rebate schemes and advice and advocacy (eg. Greenwich, Chapter Three).
- Setting up local 'one stop shop fronts' for local authority services and those they manage (eg. Newcastle, Chapter Four).
- Defining an economic development strategy within which to improve the employment and financial problems of vulnerable people (Chapter Four).
- Encouraging each department to define an anti-poverty strategy for itself and identify issues of inter-departmental importance (eg. Manchester, Chapter Three).
- Locating issues of inter-departmental concern (eg. 'debt recovery', 'under fives', 'homelessness') and organising projects with the voluntary sector and local community to address these (eg. Islington, Chapter Three).
- Assessing levels of fees and charges across departments and producing a coherent, authority-wide policy on these (Chapter Four).
- Evaluating the terms and conditions of local authority employees and improving these (eg. Manchester, Chapter Three).
- Enforcing existing equal opportunities policies more vigorously, particularly for ethnic minorities and women, and ensuring that the relationship of these to anti-poverty work is recognised (Chapter Three).
- Holding 'anti-poverty' meetings to raise consciousness of the problems of poverty and develop networks of individuals committed to supporting the strategy (Chapter Two).

3. The location of an anti-poverty strategy

Within the machinery of local government there is however no ideal location for an anti-poverty strategy. Though frequently to be found with a basis in welfare rights, an anti-poverty strategy runs the risk of being marginalised by other departments when closely linked to social security issues. The same could be said of an anti-poverty strategy based in a social services department. Yet, whilst requiring a central focus, placing an anti-poverty strategy within a chief executive's department could lead to its bureaucratic paralysis and its policies being ignored elsewhere in the authority. In any event, an entirely 'in-house' strategy, with no outside links, looks unlikely to succeed.

Although there is no ideal place in present local government structures for such a strategy, the recent interest exhibited in anti-poverty work by economic development units and their sub-committees, particularly in combatting poverty through local economic wealth creation initiatives, suggests one possible location. Placing anti-poverty strategy within economic development would in one go challenge conventional divisions between 'economic' and 'social' policy-making, and place anti-poverty action where the real causes of poverty – unemployment, low pay, low benefits and discrimination – could be given focus. There is, however, no blue-print for anti-poverty action and each local authority has to take account of its own, unique structural arrangements in deciding where to base its strategy. In the long run also, it must be recognised that structural solutions are no substitute for a sound and shared philosophy.

It is not clear at this stage of thought just how anti-poverty action might fit into service committees' work. Certainly there would have to be formal links with other departments. These could be forged through, for example, a liaison development officer plus support staff being appointed to each major service department; district health authorities and major voluntary organisations might follow suit. Secondly, an anti-poverty issues' section could be established on each major service department's agenda. Thirdly a 'poverty commentary' could become a regular discussion feature of all major items on major committees' agendas – in much the same way as 'equalities issues' are expected to be highlighted at the moment. All the above measures, however, rely on a pro-active, neo-corporate approach shared by all services and committees intent on anti-poverty action, as 'poverty awareness.'

Many of the problems for all these activities stem not from location, but from their status within the local authority's budget. In the past anti-poverty strategies have largely lacked direct funding and been supported by seconding staff and providing resources from other departments. In the future, taking anti-poverty strategy seriously will have to involve proper financing of the activities it generates if they are to have a serious impact.

4. The challenge to local government

The development of anti-poverty strategy in the 1980s has been part of a movement, based mainly in Labour authorities but also in some non-Labour ones, to broaden the role of local government and to respond more effectively to the changing needs of individuals and communities. It flies in the face, however, of current central government pressures threatening both local government finance and the delivery of services in the major and traditional areas of social services, housing and education. In the early 1990s, as a result of these pressures, local government is widely expected to undergo unprecedented change, with a drastic reduction in both its levels of expenditure and numbers of employees and a contraction of direct service provision. Such change poses a real threat to the vulnerable groups of people for whom anti-poverty strategies are designed.

Changes in both the financial and managerial structure of local government are at the forefront of this revolution. The introduction of the community charge (poll tax) in April 1990, the subsequent reform of non-domestic rates and the revision of the rate support grant as revenue support will all contribute to a curtailing of local authority finances. To raise income, authorities will have to increase their poll tax demands, thus penalising those to whom they wish to deliver improved services. The burden of poll tax payments, it is feared, will rest particularly heavily on vulnerable tenants in both council and privately rented accommodation who were previously exempt from the payment of rates. (*AMA 1989*) (*Appendix 3.*)

The extension of compulsory competitive tendering (CCT), under the Local Government Act 1988, for building cleaning, welfare and other catering, refuse collection and street cleaning, vehicle repair and maintenance, grounds maintenance and leisure management, challenges the role of local authorities as the direct providers of services. This strategy will be further extended, moreover, when the White Paper on the Griffiths Report on Community Care is implemented in 1991 under the NHS/Community Care Bill, with the consequent pressure to contract out major sections of the personal social services. Recent experience has suggested that private sector interest in the first group of services listed is limited, with many private firms put off by the high standards of service required by councils, and authorities winning their first tenders with little or no competition (*Courcouf, 1989*). It cannot be assumed, however, that this state of affairs will continue, nor that the

Department of the Environment will not press its case through issuing new guidelines on authorities' tendering procedures. Indeed, the experience of the personal social services with the rapid expansion of private residential care since the Residential Homes Act 1984 suggests that, given appropriate incentives by central government, the private sector can and will make a rapid response. Great concern is being voiced, therefore, over the effect that CCT can have on the quality of services provided, as well as over the attendant loss of protection for workers once afforded by 'contract compliance'.

The major changes anticipated in social services departments in the light of the implementation of the Griffiths Report are likely to lead firstly to a reduction in direct service provision and secondly to a restructuring of management to take account of the administrative, registration and inspectorate duties required to control extended provision from both voluntary and private sectors. The huge problem will be to ensure that the quality of caring services delivered to particularly vulnerable and non-vocal groups of people, such as children, people with physical and mental disabilities, mentally ill people and elderly people, is maintained or improved whilst costs are kept to a minimum.

In education the implications of the Education Reform Act 1988 have still to be worked through. Giving schools the choice to opt out of local authority control and extending the powers of heads and governors amongst schools remaining within the local authority control are two measures which will weaken a local authority's ability to control and manage education in its area. It will make it particularly difficult for a local authority to do much to raise levels of educational opportunity in deprived inner city or outer estate areas and could result in 'sink' or 'ghetto' type schools becoming typical of those left within a local authority's own remit. In addition, the implementation of the national curriculum will leave little room for manoeuvre to meet the special needs of children from ethnic minorities, those with recurrent absences through illness or truancy and those with disabilities and learning difficulties.

In housing, major legislation throughout the decade, in particular the 1988 Housing Act and the 1989 Local Government and Housing Act, has introduced a series of highly significant changes. For example, council tenants may now transfer from council tenancy to another landlord; Housing Action Trusts (HATs) may take over and sell off council estates; private landlords have the right to provide new short-term tenancies with little protection for tenants' rights. Because these changes involve a loss of security for those renting either council or private property, as well as a certain increase in rents, they threaten again the most vulnerable sections of the community.

As if this were not enough, poor people themselves are becoming increasingly hard pressed by the changes made under the 1986 Social Security Act and under subsequent housing acts to the regulations covering eligibility for income support, family credit, community care grants, social fund loans and housing benefit. These changes have taken place during a period in which unemployment has remained close to the 2 million mark including an intractable core of long term unemployed people, and countless in employment are struggling on unacceptable levels of low pay. Thus the challenge to local authorities to alleviate poverty is multi-faceted and daunting and requires an advanced level of clear thinking, practicality and ingenuity if it is to be met by local agencies with any degree of success.

In spite of these difficulties, there is much that is positive in the current changes that are taking place both within local government itself and in the context in which it now operates. The development of the 'enabling role' of local government (*Clarke and Stewart, 1988; Ridley, 1988*) is not only extending involvement with both voluntary and private agencies but also encouraging local authorities to assume the defence and protection of service users. Given adequate resources, measures such as the NHS/Community Care Bill could create opportunities for the empowerment of individuals that have previously often gone unrecognised. Through the more careful appraisal of needs, could come 'packages of care' more closely related to individuals' own wishes. Ultimately, the universal pressure on local authorities to economise could lead to their reorganising services in a manner more suited to the 1990s with a heightened awareness of the significance of their role in anti-poverty strategy.

Appendix One

Members of the Steering Group

Chairman
Toby Harris   Chair, AMA, Social Services Committee
                     Leader, London Borough of Haringey.

Members
John Barnes   Public Protection Department, London Borough of
                     Southwark.
Saul Becker   Deputy Director, Benefits Research Unit, University
                     of Nottingham.
Geoff Fimister   Principal Welfare Rights Officer, City of Newcastle
                     upon Tyne.
Ruth Lister   Professor of Social Work, University of Bradford.
Jane Streather   Assistant Director of Social Services, City of Newcastle
                     upon Tyne.
Sue Wainwright   Department of Social Policy & Social Work, University
                     of Birmingham.
David Wells   Director of Public Protection, London Borough of
                     Southwark.
Gill Witting   Centre for the Analysis of Social Policy, University of
                     Bath.

Secretariat
Peter Westland
Brian Jones
Susan Balloch

Appendix Two

Authorities participating in the AMA Poverty Survey

Barking & Dagenham	Hackney	Rochdale
Barnet	Hammersmith	Salford
Barnsley	Hounslow	Sandwell
Birmingham	Islington	Sefton
Bolton	Kirklees	Sheffield
Bradford	Knowsley	Solihull
Brent	Lambeth	South Tyneside
Bury	Leeds	Southwark
Calderdale	Lewisham	Stockport
Coventry	Manchester	Sunderland
Doncaster	Newcastle	Tameside
Dudley	North Tyneside	Wigan
Gateshead	Oldham	Wolverhampton
Greenwich		

Other passenger transport and fire authorities participating included:

Greater Manchester	Passenger Transport Authority County Fire Service
Merseyside	Passenger Transport Authority Fire and Civil Defence Authority
Tyne and Wear	Passenger Transport Authority Metropolitan Fire Brigade
South Yorkshire Joint Authority	
West Midlands	Passenger Transport Authority Fire Authority

Appendix Three:

Anti-poverty Strategies
Taken from 'Collecting the Community Charge: Choices for Local Authorities'
published by Association of Metropolitan Authorities

The introduction of poll tax will cause further hardship for people experiencing poverty. Even those on income support will have to pay at least 20% of the tax. Although the Government has gone some way towards raising income support levels to enable people to meet this additional commitment, in many areas the extra amount will not be sufficient to meet the 20% of the poll tax demand.

This guide highlights a number of areas where authorities have the choice between providing a mechanism service or a sensitive service which takes account of an individual's circumstances.

Essentially these choices, whether they are about promoting take up campaigns for rebates or about operating a sensitive recovery service, relate to the recognition and alleviation of poverty. At the same time it must be recognised that there is a significant additional cost to providing a sensitive service.

Authorities also need to consider the effect that decisions taken about poll tax will have on other services. A rigid debt recovery policy which takes no account of an individual's ability to pay may well produce results as far as the collection of poll tax is concerned. However, this may be at the expense of non-payment of the rent or as a result of borrowing money from a loan shark.

In the longer term a hard line approach to debt recovery may well lead to an increase in homelessness, marital breakups, etc. These may in turn lead to increased costs to the authority. Therefore, rather than take decisions about poll tax in isolation it is recommended that they are made within the framework of an anti-poverty strategy.

Anti-poverty strategies are essentially about:

The provision of services on the basis of need rather than income.

The maximisation of basic income levels, especially for those dependent on benefits and the low waged.

Economic development and the creation of jobs in the area.

The collection and recovery of debts and charges in as sensitive a manner as possible.

An example of one authority's anti-poverty strategy is attached.

An essential component of any anti-poverty strategy is a clear, authority wide policy covering debt recovery. Although the majority of people in debt have multiple debt problems, the local authority is often the single biggest creditor. Even though there are different legal remedies for different categories of debts it is important that the authority has a consistent policy on the treatment of those in debt.

Debt recovery procedures

The following set of objectives for a debt recovery policy are taken from the joint report of the National Consumer Council and Welsh Consumer Council *Consumers and Debt* (1983):

Debt recovery procedures must:

be sufficiently effective to ensure that – whenever they have the means – people do pay their debts and are not able to avoid their obligations;

acknowledge the debtor's obligations to his/her dependents;

distinguish whenever possible between those who cannot pay their debts and those who will not pay them;

allow for the proper consideration of a debtor's circumstances and provide sensible arrangements for those that genuinely need time to pay their debts;

protect debtors and their families from harassment and undue hardship;

attempt to sort out debt problems as easily as possible before they escalate out of control;

allow for the differences which exist between the well organised creditor and the badly organised debtor;

maximise the prospects of the 'rehabilitation' of debtors;

achieve a fair balance between the claims of competing creditors;

be efficient and cost effective.

These principles should enable members and officers to formulate efficient and sensitive procedures for the recovery of debts.

When putting them into practice authorities should bear in mind the following practical points. There should be:

clear, written, policy guidelines for all staff involved in cash collection and debt-recovery;

clear, written policy guidelines for bailiffs, collection agencies, etc that recover money on the authority's behalf;

easy access at every stage in the debt recovery procedure to help and advise with debts. The aim should be to identify potential problems and deal with them as soon as they arise;

clear information about the authority's recovery procedures given to individuals and advice agencies so that poll tax payers know where they stand. Where appropriate this should be translated into other languages;

consideration given to the encouragement of credit unions as an alternative source of borrowing to loan sharks.

Appendix Four:

Example of a statement of principles for one council's anti-poverty strategy

Taken from 'Collecting the Community Charge: Choices for Local Authorities' published by Association of Metropolitan Authorities

The following statement has been adopted by the council.

The city council recognises that there are a substantial number of areas where it, or indeed any local authority will have little or no impact directly on the cases and effects of poverty, and that the eradication of poverty and need can only be achieved by:

a fundamental redistribution of wealth and political and economic power;

an equitable tax and benefits system;

the development of a National Health Service and public transport system which provide accessible and comprehensive services for everyone;

the development of a comprehensive energy policy which does not cause hardship;

the council will use what influence it has to work for these ends.

Nonetheless an important contribution can be made. As far as the council's own direct functions are concerned the city council is committed to:

ensuring, as far as possible, that an individual's level of income does not affect their ability to participate in decisions about issues which affect them.

the provisions of services on the basis of need rather than income;

ensuring that individuals and groups are not stigmatised because of low income;

the collection of outstanding debts and charges in as sensitive a manner as possible to ensure that further hardship, distress or financial difficulties are not created;

the maximisation of individual income levels wherever possible, especially for those dependent on benefits and the low waged, through comprehensive provision of information, advice and the prompt, sensitive and accurate administration of benefits;

a programme of education and information aimed at raising the level of awareness amongst the public at large, individuals, groups and communities, about the extent of poverty, its origins and effects and possible remedies;

providing skills training and encouragement to those in need, in order to enable them to speak for themselves, and to overcome their experience of dependency and powerlessness;

ensuring that the benefits arising from capital investment and revenue expenditure by the council accrue to those in greatest need.

All departments of the council will be examining their services against these principles and in four aspects proposing action to:

make services at least equally accessible to people experiencing poverty, but adopting positive action to target services towards low income groups where appropriate;

review objectives to ensure that the needs of people experiencing poverty are adequately taken into account;

review whether people experiencing poverty are actually receiving services and benefitting appropriately and reviewing the impact of service upon poverty;

ensuring that there is an accurate understanding of poverty eg through consultation with people, surveys, training of workers and management.

Bibliography

Abel Smith B. and Townsend P., 1965, *The Poor and the Poorest*, G. Bell & Sons.

Association of Metropolitan Authorities, 1987, *Greater London Housing Condition Survey*, AMA, 35 Great Smith Street, SW1P 3BJ.

Association of Metropolitan Authorities, 1988, *Housing and HIV Infection*, The Local Authority Associations' Officer Working Group on AIDS, AMA.

Association of Metropolitan Authorities, Association of County Councils, 1988, *Social Fund – Practice Guide and Position Statement.*

Association of Metropolitan Authorities, 1989, *Collecting the Community Charge*, AMA.

Association of Metropolitan Authorities, 1989, *Community Development, the Local Authority Role*, AMA.

Association of Metropolitan Authorities, 1989, *HIV Infection and the Workplace*, The Local Authority Associations' Officer Working Group on AIDS, AMA.

Archbishop of Canterbury's Commission on Urban Priority Areas, 1986, *Faith in the City*, Church House.

Audit Commission, 1989, *Housing the Homeless: the Local Authority Role*, HMSO Books.

Balloch S., Hume C., Jones B. and Westland P., 1985, *Caring for Unemployed People: A Study of the Impact of Unemployment on Demand for Personal Social Services*, Bedford Square Press, AMA.

Balloch S. and Jones B., 1988, *Social Services Responses to Poverty*, in Public Issues, Private Pain, Becker S. & MacPherson S. eds., Care Matters Ltd., Insight.

Becker S. and MacPherson S., 1986, *Poor Clients: The Extent and Nature of Financial Poverty*

Amongst Consumers of Social Work Services, Nottingham University, Benefits Research Unit.

Becker S., 1989, *Vulnerable Clients: The Findings of the First Case Review Snapshot*, University of Nottingham, Research Report SFP 3.89.

Becker S., 1989, *Small Change: Findings from the third Referral Snapshot and Second Case Review Exercise*, Benefits Research Unit, University of Nottingham, Social Services Research Group.

Beresford D. and Croft S., 1986, *Whose Welfare – Private Care or Public Services?*, Lewis Cohen, Urban Studies Centre, Brighton.

Berthoud R., Brown J. C. and Cooper S., 1981, *Poverty and the Development of Anti-Poverty Policy in the United Kingdom*, Heinemann Educational Books.

Berthoud R., 1984, *Reform of Supplementary Benefit* (Working Papers, Vols. 1 & 2), Policy Studies Institute.

Berthoud, R., Benson S. and Williams S., 1986, *Standing Up for Claimants: Welfare Rights Work in Local Authorities*, Policy Studies Institute Research Report No. 663.

Berthoud R., 1989, *Credit, Debt and Poverty*, HMSO, Social Security Advisory Committee, Research Paper 1.

Berthoud R. and Hinton T., 1989, *Credit Unions in the United Kingdom*, Policy Studies Institute.

Blom Cooper L., 1985, *A Child in Trust*, London Borough of Brent, Kingswood Press.

Bradshaw J. and Holmes H., 1989, *Living on the Edge: A Study of the Living Standards of Families on Benefit in Tyne and Wear*, Tyneside C.P.A.G.

Bramley G., Le Grand J. and Low W., 1989, *How Far is the Poll Tax a 'Community Charge'? The Implications of Service Usage?*, London School of Economics, The Welfare State Programme ST/ICERD, Discussion Paper IOSP/42, April 1989.

British Medical Association, 1987, *Deprivation and Ill Health*, B.M.A., Board of Science and Education Discussion Paper.

Chandler, Chapman and Hollington, *Fire Incidence, Housing and Social Conditions – The Urban Situation in Britain*, Fire Prevention, No. 172.

Cheetham, J., 1982, *Social Work and Ethnicity*, Allen & Unwin.

Clarke M. and Stewart J., 1988, *The Enabling Authority*, Local Government Training Board.

Cleveland County Council Welfare Rights Services, 1989, *For Richer, For Poorer*, Welfare Rights Services, Middlesbrough, Cleveland.

Coates K. and Silburn R., 1970, *Poverty: The Forgotten Englishmen*, Penguin Books, Harmondsworth.

Courcouf L., 1989, *Compulsory Competitive Tendering – So Far So Good?*, Municipal Review, No. 698, June 1989.

Department of Employment Gazette, 1988, *Ethnic Origins and the Labour Market*, D. of E. Gazette, December, 1988.

DHSS, 1985, *Low Income Families*.

DHSS, 1985, *Households Below Average Income: A Statistical Analysis 1981–1985*.

Disability Alliance, 1987, *Poverty and Disability: Breaking the Link*, Disability Alliance.

Disability Alliance Era, 1989, *Disability Rights Handbook, 14th Edition, April 1989–April 1990*, The Disability Alliance Era, 25 Denmark Street, London WC2H 8NJ.

Dominelli L., 1989, *Anti-racist Social Work*, BASW/MacMillan.

Donnison, D., 1988, *Defining and Measuring Poverty: A Reply to Stein Ringen*, Journal of Social Policy, Volume 17, Part 3, July 1988.

Esam P. and Oppenheim C., 1989, *A Charge on the Community: The Poll Tax, Benefits and the Poor*, CPAG/LGIU.

Evans F., 1989, *Decentralisation and Newcastle*, Unpublished Paper for Newcastle City Council.

Field F., 1989, *Losing Out: The Emergence of Britain's Underclass*, Basil Blackwell.

Fimister G., 1986, *Welfare Rights Work in Social Services*, B.A.S.W.

Flynn P., 1986, *Urban Deprivation: What it is and How to Measure it*, Public Money, September 1986.

Gibbons J., 1989, *Helping Poor Families with Pre-School Services*, Social Work Today, 1st June 1989, Vol. 20, No. 38 pp. 15–17.

Goldberg E. M. and Warburton R. W., 1979, *Ends & Means in Social Work*, National Institute for Social Work, London.

Griffiths R., 1988, *Community Care – Agenda For Action*, HMSO.

Hibbitt J., 1988, *Welfare in Lambeth in the 1980s*, Unpublished M.A. Dissertation, Department of Social Science and Administration, Goldsmiths College.

Hoggett P. and Hambleton R. (eds.), 1987, *Decentralisation and Democracy: Localising Public Services*, University of Bristol School for Advanced Urban Studies.

Jarman B., 1983, *Identification of Underprivileged Areas*, British Medical Journal, Vol. 286.

Jarman B., 1984, *Underprivileged Areas: Validation and Distribution of Scores*, British Medical Journal, Vol. 289.

Johnson P. and Webb S., 1989, *'Counting People with Low Incomes' The Impact of Recent Changes in Official Statistics*, Institute for Fiscal Studies.

Jones B., 1989, *Section One at the Crossroads?*, 'Benefits Research', Issue Three, Nottingham Benefits Research Unit.

Lewis O., 1961, *The Children of Sanchez*, Random House, New York.

Lewis O., 1966, *La Vida*, Random House, New York.

Mack J. and Lansley S., 1984, *Poor Britain*, Allen & Unwin.

Martin J. and Roberts C., 1984, *Women and Employment: A Lifetime Perspective*, The Report of the 1980 DE/OPCS Women and Employment Survey, HMSO.

Millar J. and Glendinning C., 1989, *Gender and Poverty*, The Journal of Social Policy, Volume 18, Part 3, July 1989.

Moore J. (Secretary of State for Social Security), 11th May 1989, Speech to the Conservative Political Centre.

Murray C., 1989, *Underclass*, Sunday Times Magazine, 26th November 1989.

Newman C., 1989, *Young Runaways*, The Children's Society.

Office of Population, Censuses and Surveys (O.P.C.S.), 1988, 1989, *Surveys of Disability in Great Britain* (Reports 1–6), HMSO.

Oppenheim C., 1988, *Poverty: The Facts*, C.P.A.G.

Osborne A. F. and Millbank J. E., 1987, *The Effects of Early Education*, Oxford, Clarendon Press.

Potter T., 1989, *Back from the Brink: Low Pay and Local Authority Anti-Poverty Strategies*, West Midlands Low Pay Unit.

Randall G., 1989, *Homeless and Hungry – A Sign of the Times*, Centrepoint, Soho.

Ridley N., 1988, *The Local Right: Enabling Not Providing*, Centre for Policy Studies, Policy Study No. 92.

Ringen S., 1988, *Direct and Indirect Measures of Poverty* (Discussion with David Donnison), Journal of Social Policy, Volume 17, Part 3, July 1988.

Seebohm F., 1968, *Report of the Committee on Local Authority and Allied Personal Social Services*, Cmnd. 3707, HMSO.

Sellgren J., 1987, *Local Economic Development and Local Initiatives in the Mid-1980s*, Local Government Studies, November/December 1987.

Short Report, 1984, *Children in Care Volume One* (Report of the Social Services Committee), HMSO.

Southwark Borough Council, 1989, *Broken Promises: The Southwark Experience of the London Docklands Development Corporation*, Southwark Borough Council.

Stewart G. and Stewart J., 1988, *Shifting the Safety Net*, in Becker S. and MacPherson S. (eds.), *Public Issues, Private Pain*, Care Matters Ltd.

Stewart G., Stewart J. and Walker C., 1989, *The Social Fund: A Critical Analysis of its Introduction and First Year in Operation*, Association of County Councils.

Stewart J. (ed.), 1989, *Welfare Rights Work in Social Work Education*, CCETSW Paper 28.1.

Stewart J., 1983, *Local Government: The Conditions of Local Choice*, Allen & Unwin.

Stoker G., 1988, *The Politics of Local Government*, MacMillan Education.

Taylor D., 1987, *Living with Unemployment*, in Walker & Walker eds.

Thane P., 1982, *The Foundations of the Welfare State*, Longman.

Thunhurst C., 1985, *Poverty and Health in the City of Sheffield*, Sheffield City Polytechnic for the Environmental Health Dept., Sheffield City Council.

Townsend P., 1979, *Poverty in the United Kingdom*, Penguin Books.

Townsend P. and Davidson N., 1982, *Inequalities in Health Care – The Black Report*, Penguin Books.

Townsend P., Simpson D. and Tibbs N., 1984, *Inequalities of Health in the City of Bristol*, Department of Social Administration, University of Bristol.

Townsend P., Corrigan P. and Kowarzik U., 1987, *Poverty and Labour in London*, Low Pay Unit.

Townsend P., 1988, *Inner City Deprivation and Premature Death in Greater Manchester*, Tameside MBC.

Walker A. and Walker C. (eds.), 1987, *The Growing Divide: A Social Audit 1979–1987*, C.P.A.G.

Whitehead M., 1987, *The Health Divide*, Health Education Council.

Willmott P., 1989, *Community Initiatives, Patterns and Prospects*, Policy Studies Institute.

Appendix to Chapter Two

Local Poverty Profiles and Related Local Studies

Birmingham	Poverty in Birmingham	1989
Bradford	Bradford in Figures	1984
	District Trends	1984
	Poverty, Health and Disadvantage	1987
Camden	Camden Survey of People with Disabilities and Long Term Health Problems	1988
Coventry	Beyond the Brink (Low Pay Unit)	1989
Greenwich	Breadline Greenwich	1984
	Areas of Stress in Greenwich	1985
Lambeth	Deprivation and Poverty in Lambeth	1986
	Lambeth Social Audit (Nathaniel Lichfield and Partners)	1987
	Lambeth Housing Needs Survey	1986
Lewisham	A Social Atlas of Poverty in Lewisham (Centre of Inner City Studies, Goldsmiths College, University of London)	1989
Manchester	Poverty in Manchester	1986
	Poverty in Manchester: The Third Investigation	1989
	Road Accidents to Children in Manchester (Sub-Group of the Black Report Working Party on Accidents to Children)	1987

Sheffield	Review of the Areas of Poverty in Sheffield	1987
	Poverty and Health in the City of Sheffield	1985
	(Colin Thunhurst, Sheffield City Polytechnic)	
Southwark	Fair Shares? The Southwark Poverty Profile	1987
	Southwark's Health	1987
Tameside	The Black Elderly in Tameside	1987
Wigan	'Wigan's Council Estates: A Report on Housing Stress and Social Hardship'	1986